The Duke of Doucheville

Meth or My Daughter

...A Memoir by Some Guy

Matthew Garon

CONTENTS

DEDICATIONS

*This book is dedicated to Evelyn, first and foremost – I see you, and I know you see me.

It's also dedicated to my poor girlfriend, Tammy, who had to read this debacle as I was writing it, and to my family - who may have taken time off for their safety, but never left me.

*It is also dedicated to all those humans that purchased Alanis Morisette's single, "Isn't it Ironic," and were clever enough to realize that none of her examples of irony are actually ironic.

1 | THE PURPOSE AND PLIGHT-
NOVEMBER 20TH, 2021

I am the product of self-will run riot, and my payback to this big blue ball called Earth seems to be a penance that I haven't the stones to endure. At least not yet…it's really not that dramatic to most, nor should it be…but it's been the one compelling area of defeat that I have repeatedly suffered. Fatherhood.

I've never been one for losing. In fact, I'm pretty sure I have a lifetime record of winning all things competitive or "winnable" in the ninety percent range. I don't have the statistics to show you, but I can recall almost every sober day of my life and most of the fucked up ones. Some more vivid than others. I just won't do shit I suck at, and I don't suck at much. Sounds douche-y, I know…but look, I used to think I sucked at parenting. There are no statistics for that one. The intense ball of hot mess chef and, at times, single dad that is me, compounded by the ferocity in my words coming at you that eerily compares to that of some of death row's finest psychopaths. I'm just too intense for full time friendships, I can humbly admit, and I fully accept this. I know me, unfortunately. I can't get out, I've tried. I'll never be a coward to my own self-pity. I can fail every day of my life, but knowing there is a ten year old beating heart out there that needs me alive......saves me.

It's about my kid. It's Evelyn, my daughter, and the purity of my life through our happiness. It's her abduction...again.

It's my inability to keep her, yes, physically keep her without having someone, be it DCF, her mom, grandma, fake Austrian dad, auntie-antichrist, uncle vanilla shit, or insert self-righteous, boundary-overstepping cunt. You can probably see my point, I'm sure. If you can't, best pick up a different book- you've already supported my cause and there is nothing left to gain from my arrogance and insipid thoughts and deplorable behaviors. Furthermore, Americans have been sold the 'see something, say something' plan, and sales are at an all-time record high. You may have purchased some of this ridiculous notion, so, once again, I implore you to put this down. What people should be buying more of in order to align themselves with their own souls is a giant glass of irrelevance and shut the fuck up. Sales are so high in minding the fuck out of everyone else's business that I can't even get high without one of said obstacles getting in our happy way. See, now we're stuck with each other. Let's go!

It's my active and inactive meth addiction and my sobriety. It's times when I'm not sure I'm two-footed in either, and not sure in which state I was meant to even exist.

It's my insistence that there isn't a rule on Earth that was geared towards my compliance or expecting of it otherwise.

It's my lust for this kid's success. It's my blood, which I would offer her as freely as my every effort, sober or not. There isn't a noun on Earth I wouldn't run through for her.

It's my purpose. She, Evelyn, is my sole purpose.

It's the fact that I check in as a dad every day and that makes me happy. It gives me and my core a sense of fulfillment in the moment. Gratitude is unavoidable. It makes Evelyn happy because she knows I'm not qualified, but she keeps me appearing "qualified" because she loves me like a real dad and sees my efforts. I am a real dad, sometimes. She pees in a cup for me to help me pass drug tests, she apologizes for me, she covers my ass...because I cover hers. She's only ten years old. A bit overqualified for life at ten, most would agree. Am I a real dad? Not like this. I can recite the words to being a real dad that I hear on television or throughout observing life day-to-day, but being accountable by more than just your biological obligations and paternity is nothing to celebrate. It's fucking normal. We applaud dads for being present when I'm not sure how they got let off the proverbial hooks for being otherwise. It's fucking irritating the support from people, albeit well intended, that celebrate parents doing regular shit that should need no acknowledgment, yet our culture dictates it does and puts each accountable dad on a pedestal. Keep me off yours. I'm on Evelyn's and looking to get off of there too. The only place to go from a pedestal is down. FYI.

It's me not ever overthinking how I'm doing as a dad and having the authentic purpose in my heart and in my actions, and most surprisingly, in my words and in my restraint.

It's that we need each other, Evelyn and I. She's the sloppy slice of life I need in the worst way, and I'm the person on her perpetually growing pedestal without any other reason other than I love and listen. I show up. I speak up. I put up - all for her. And I don't do that for anyone. I mean, I dishonestly whispered such nonsense in the ears of girlfriends past, but that was just to maintain the quid pro quo balance and get some ass. Evelyn and I actually need each other.

Oh, so whole point of this story is that Evelyn's been taken, again. Like, parent-to-parent kidnapped by her mother in Thailand on her latest chaperoned vacation back there, again. Without warning or discussion, again. Days before fifth grade was about to start and right on the heels of a little league championship and a fourth grade spelling bee title. Damn it! We were doing it. I couldn't believe it was finally working, but it was. In spite of the facts as to who I am as a human, Evelyn and I share something I can't explain. She and I just know each other. She tries to see everything good in me even when I'm at my worst. There's a magnetism between us; an organic love. It's fucking awesome. It's a bond most people would describe with a massive hint of jealousy in their tone. We take that as a compliment.

Her mother is far from dumb and stoic as a bust, so I can only speculate as to the reason for her abduction this time. I imagine it's the fact that in the three years since she's moved to the States with me (one of which was clouded in active meth addiction and the next year being a mediocre dad at best with intermittent relapses) we have developed an unconditional, restraining-order-worthy relationship built out of imperfect love and trust and unequivocal support, that she's became so overly filled with mind-fucked-rage that she lost it and vanished because it's the only thing she knows. I remember the day Evelyn was born in Cebu, Philippines and I told her mother I was going to be this kid's total dude - her hero, her everything. Her mother refuted my ability to be that then. Who's to say she feels differently today? Could be a lot of things, but the reason is not the point. The point is the point, and the point reeks of mental instability. I have no PhD, but I have a nose for people with something not right. I actually left college after three semesters with a point-three-seven GPA. A PhD wasn't in the cards, not with that shitty GPA. I'm not waiting three and a half years again to see my daughter. That is my only never again.

Last time she was abducted, for lack of a better word, I could see that leaving Annie, Evelyn's mother, stranded with my Evelyn in the Philippines while I was high on ice…meth, while not being shy nor cleverly evasive about the revolving door of eighteen-year-old prostitutes that I preferred to fuck over her, may have fueled her decision to vanish. Or it could have been the zero nights I spent with her after Evelyn was born for the first three months of her life while she adjusted to her first experience living in a foreign country. Not to mention I was off getting accolades and world nominations for food art I didn't even create. Maybe it was the fact that I scolded her for having a ceremony on our wedding night instead of just signing the damn paper like I asked. I left just after our Bangkok nuptials to get some drugs and ass while she entertained my brother and sister during their second night outside of the US ever. I took the money envelopes from our bullshit wedding that night too. We cut our "honeymoon" short due to not having that money, and I never felt an ounce of guilt about it. Weird. I resented knocking up my dog-walker and took it out on Evelyn. I resented losing my super hot girlfriend. I never resented being a father. I never wanted to be a husband. I imposed my self-will in the matter of the safety of my own child. I didn't realize this until a few years later.

All I know is that it's going to be hard to convince anyone that I'm a "good person" from this point on, but I can't seem to be ok with removing her as she did me from Evelyn's life. Maybe it's just dumb. It is dumb, but I can't change. It's dumb not to at least prepare for it, and I was left slack-jawed once again. Fool me twice, shame on me...bullshit. At least not allowing that again and taking preparations to see through her return would have been wise, seeing as the first go-round was the catalyst for this salty white, crusty head I inherited over the years, compiled with countless moments of piercing heartache, not to mention a prescription of Ambien to cope and habits to just about any mood or mind altering chemical out there. Real pain. I always justified Evelyn's mom doing what she did because of said facts and during the first round of "Evelyn abduction." Seeing as Evelyn wasn't old enough to speak, and I really didn't know what to do as a dad, I ultimately preferred that it be Evelyn's choice in whom she lets fuck up her life... dad or mom. I loved her and wanted her, but it scared me. A lot. I was a pussy for not working harder, but I swore I would never do that again. Did I? I can't say I did, but I can't say I didn't. I did say I would only have one 'never again'...

Hence, round two. And, thus, writing becomes my beacon when all I am left with are my own rotten thoughts in the absence of my child and her whereabouts. The emptiness hits me like a duck getting horse pegged as I sprawl across the only empty set of seats on my 777. I'm flying back to Boston empty-hearted, empty soul-ed, empty, empty. Sure, social media friends rip off condolences to help me through, and it truly does, because I'm sober and not angered. They don't get that good dads don't lose their kids. I know the reality, but I accept the condolences and even compliments. I try to keep a red heart…it's been working. I read the Tao, but that only lasts with constant immersion and practice and, let's be real, for a guy like me that was born with a black heart and speckled soul - it is almost impossible to sustain practicing, nevermind master!.

I can fill myself with daily bullshit that my purpose, my reason for being, serves one greater purpose than that of anyone I know or ever have known. Stupid, right? It is, don't answer that. You'll sound as dumb as I do. Half the shit I say I think almost immediately, "What the fuck are you on about, bruh?"

I, like every other human, am an emotional tool. Guilty. A misunderstood being that just needs to be heard. An overlooked superstar that never got his chance. I lack the ability to keep that tool as sharp as most people. Fuck, I lack a lot of tools. My toolbox has a lot of blunt objects dulled by the inability to execute my own life through my own eyes in a way that makes me wake up with a contented heart and all the feels of a guy that has met his potential "purpose."

I remember reading a book some years back. Yeah, I did that once. I've actually read a few, but honestly just a couple front to back. The book was called Outliers and I remember so vividly the parts that pertain to my internal assessment of MY own greatness, as I saw it. My thing was people. It still is. It may be because my "thing" isn't an average financial acumen or semblance of life stability, so my fallback is people. It's nothing more than a default for most ignoramus', but it almost excused me from having to answer to my lack of professionalism, emotional, intimate, or long-term structural success in my own life, or through the eyes of my parents or peers. I am as raw and detestable as a person gets when it comes to my words, yet as kind and well-aimed as anyone when it comes to my actions (please refer to sober me, only). I am without apology a bitter pill to swallow, and if swallowed, I may just kill you. More drama, I know. Fact is, I just don't have any idea how I come across to others at times, nor do I give a fuck. I do care that whomever I like, or even those I don't, takes something away from the experience of meeting me. Anyway, back to that book I read. It was the chapter in that book that spoke to the direct correlation between a person's success and their ability to coerce and manipulate the people they surrounded themselves with into the most fortuitous and self-serving environment possible that made me tick. If the guy that led the Manhattan project was so fucking charming and could get himself excused at an attempt at his own father's life but the intellectually smartest man on earth couldn't talk his way back into community college because of a mere formality, then the answer was crystal clear: be the first guy. The ability to be a salesman, confidant, liaison, spokesperson, and bestie to anyone I saw fit has been the one true reason I have even had a modicum of success in this world. It always will be.

My career as a chef has spanned through Boston, Singapore, Thailand, and the Philippines. I call it a career, but it has really just served as my hobby while I fit the rest of my fast life into that bubble. When my life bubble gets too big and too fast, I find another schmuck to hire me and pay me enough for my next adventure. I implode, self-destruct, and repeat after gaining some semblance of being employable or trustworthy once again. Proudly, I get that feeling as if I've pulled the wool over another idiot's eyes, because I have. Ultimately, my goal - no, my intention - is to give back to humans. Like them or hate them, I feel some clandestine purpose to rip their existence to shreds by finding their point of contraction in their purported integrity and help them figure it out from there, and then get on with my own self. The benefit others feel I gain from this is theirs, not mine. Sometimes I sugarcoat my experiences as if there is a need, as if anyone else really gives a fuck about whether I lived in three or one hundred and fifty-three countries they have never experienced. It's natural for us to want to paint our life's journey and accomplishments with a rose-colored brush, but it'll never be anything more than a tire-pumping exercise in narcissism. It, meaning my professional career, has been defined as a complete failure in respect to what most see as my potential, but I think it's quite common (or at least more often than not) in people these days. There, that made me feel better. Phew! I don't forgive or excuse my own failures, but fuck, there is nothing I would or could do differently. I am me. I read a quote recently. I am glad the author was unknown, so I don't have to credit anyone else in my own book. The quote smacked me upside my noggin, "Someone once asked, 'Why must you always choose the most difficult path?' I answered, 'Why do you presume that I see two paths?' That was it. I see one and only one. I will always see one. I am a man of impulse and if you don't like it, I will find someone who will. It's not going to go well for me by repeating the same mistakes fueled by platinum intentions ...that's how I got to this point in the first place.

I read these memes on social media about inspiration and self-worth, and I think that if I ever need to wake up and download an app that becomes necessary for me to feel better about myself in any given day, then the party is over. I may as well grab the first firearm I find (which I've always wanted to own) and pull the trigger. Then I start to digress into thoughts of missing and being a vegetable or some shit and ultimately end up thinking about whether or not they'll give me an electric wheelchair that propels me fast enough to hurl my body over the edge of a cliff. This seems way more enjoyable than thinking about making notes about the arbitrary bullshit I "need" to do today or finding solace in online dating or going through perceived acceptable stages of life based on the social practices of whatever plot of land I happen to currently occupy by the same groups of people I get nauseated in being around. I try to avoid self-loathing and, as I call it, "uppity-cuntishness" because I know what that looks like from the other side. Ew.

Recently, I decided to self-implode…. again. This is the story of my life when there is even the mention of Matt Garon having some success. Anyway, I recently received an email from the lawyer that represented my most recent former employer, reciting the words I used, "uppity-cunt," as the reason in her email about why I could no longer communicate directly with the cunts in their HR department. They were cunts. I mean, I had a relapse after thirty days of ass-kissing training with a corporate, fast casual concept out of NYC that assessed a person's character during the training process as if we were subject to termination for not smiling and saying "welcome" when someone came through the door for a twelve-dollar box of dead animals served over dead plants and obliterated grains. Anyone would relapse after that, but I was a parent and the thought of somehow inserting myself into life's timeline as an "appropriate" parent must have made me fucking insane to the point where an ounce of crystal meth and a revolving door of questionable hookers seemed like a good idea at the time. The email hit me though as another sparkling moment of clarity in another culmination of self-inflicted defeat.

That great idea of picking up a bag of crystallized methamphetamine (said no human ever), my beautiful and fantastical shards once again, all because I deserved it, has now led to me chasing my ten-year-old child, my actual purpose, around Southeast Asia while her cunt-of-a-mother stays one step ahead. I guess I never weigh consequences. I weigh instant gratification. I weigh truth. I weigh intent. I weigh excitement and stimulation. I weigh my ego. My ego tips the scales of all those other things combined, yet I never weigh what other people are doing, and for that, I am grateful....

The one thing I do, or at least keep true in my heart involuntarily, is love the fuck out of my kid. I can't explain it, as no parent can. Articulation of words is useless because it will never place a mark on the reality of the feeling we experience. Evelyn is mine, or at least she should be and wants to be, but she is currently owned and operated by a Thai puppet she involuntarily calls Mom. She came into the scene after I decided that while dating a seventeen-year-old Thai model and making a nice home with her, that I would add some risk and excitement to my already overstimulated existence and ninety-hour work week and fuck my dog-walker and seafood rep. Her name, as I mentioned, is Annie, and she rightfully owns the purple devil emoji with the upside-down smile in my phone these days, as well as custodial rights to Evelyn in Thailand. This was only due to my poor negotiating skills during our uncontested divorce that I, in desperation, with a promise of 'never again', regretfully signed when Evelyn was four years old. I'll never regret choosing my daughter's happiness over a piece of paper. She will own that emoji forever. I think now, being on my second tour of parent abduction in a third world country, she has earned the emoji. She is the sole human out of over eight billion plus known to exist that I can say that with absolute confidence I would be happier if she were less alive, like dead. That will never change. You can throw in my sister-in-law to that list now that I'm being completely honest too. My sister-in-law is actually not even emoji worthy. Not until they make poop on a burning pile of rubber while getting ass-raped by methheads in Worcester, MA emoji. Worcester, MA happens to be my least favorite city in the world, in case you couldn't tell.

I consider myself a forgiving and overly trusting person because ultimately, I prefer that people enjoy me and trust me, unless I can't stand you from the jump. I also feel as though me being trusting is, in fact, empowering you to trust me. I have no problem going first. Though I don't always deserve trust, it has always been an avenue of strength and hope and something that has allowed me to build the closest connections to "real" people. My people. Something my sister-in-law would know nothing about. Addicted me will take that trust and incinerate any hope of rekindling a friendship and make you ill at the thought of my face. It will tell you that straight me is here! The minute you start to gain the trust-traction - bam, your fucking nuts are in a vice on the table and your bank account is empty. Sick me. How that version of me hasn't gotten both versions killed to this point is astounding. It doesn't hurt that I have an intimidating build and impetuous mouth.

Straight me will reciprocate your returned trust tenfold. The trick is to never meet or negotiate with addicted me. I know it's an overused cliché to say, "I don't care about what you think of me," but I truly don't. The people who say they don't are the same ones that massage people's feelings with euphemisms and clutter their inboxes with apologies and self-seeking letters. They are constantly fishing for a thought, meme, hint, or emoji that helps them to understand their general fucking place in some irrelevant clown's life, not realizing that (here's another cliché) "in the grand scheme of things" it doesn't and never will matter. They are the same people that contradict themselves daily in what they purport in words as they execute in their actions or avoid in their insecurities. I care that you benefit somehow from knowing me. I care that there is no such thing as an elephant in the room. I enjoy conflict, confrontation, challenging things intellectually, challenging myself and others, physically and intellectually, and being the reason you can't sleep because there is just some intangible quality to my existence that you can't put your finger on. That is my second purpose.

2 | SINGAPORE – MARCH 2008

I remember the fear I had my first few weeks in Singapore. I remember all my sobering moments with exquisite lucidity, and most of the fucked-up ones. I remember all of Singapore, actually. I was living alone in Alina's apartment. A place we were set to rekindle our romantic flame. Actually, that was more her modus operandi than mine. My MO was making her my ex-girlfriend, soon after discovering a world of infinite beauty in Southeast Asia that I never knew existed. I was intimidated by Singapore, initially. To that point in my life, my only travel destination farther than Greater Boston was a drunken Spring Break jaunt to Negril, Jamaica.

Singapore represented a world of exotic adventure to a Boston-based meathead like myself. There were systematically developed areas throughout Singapore; Malay, Indian, Chinese, Singaporean, and Ang Mo (or yellow hair) areas. Singapore was a booming economy with infinite potential and a well-run government. It was flat as a board on a geophysical scale. Personal vehicles in Singapore were not allowed to be more than ten years old and chewing gum was prohibited; unlawful even. The government would come on your car's tenth birthday to help get rid of it if you didn't. It was strict and uptight, but it was my home, for now.

By month two I found myself living out the last few days to weeks at Alina's (my ex's) place. She was back home in the US for the summer. I had moved to Singapore to be with her just three months before and we originally planned to be together during the summer, but things usually went downhill pretty fast with me, especially in my relationships, just as soon as my current situation showed too much hope and return on my investment, or the grass seemed a little too green on the other side. I treated women as I did napkins, at the time.

The time to myself would help me to get over the relationship, financially more-so than emotionally, and process my new single life in SE Asia. I'd have the summer to get to know the entire country, which is essentially a large city. I wanted to give it a try. Singapore was considered "Asia Lite" for foreigners looking to live abroad due to the large amount of expatriates living and working there, and how widely used English was. Months earlier I had left my successful job just north of Boston, MA, and moved from the US to Singapore to be with my girlfriend, Alina, while she started work for a prestigious international school. I thought before I left Boston that we would eventually get married, but that was just a fluffed intention and symptom of my sobriety, and addiction. I was just off a life-changing award and the best stretch of authentic, sober life I had known after years of addiction and chronic relapse. Singapore was her thing. I was a complimentary piece to her life, so I always had my eyes open to life with or without her. I had been sober for three years prior to moving to Singapore, but with the thought of being alone in Singapore and my girlfriend now back to the US for a teacher's summer and me starting a new job in a new country with no one to be accountable for except myself, the thought of going back to drinking had become a perpetual thought. There was now an insatiable thirst where my addiction had laid dormant in my Alcoholics Anonymous, Big Book thumping days back in Boston.

I was starting a new job - my first job abroad. I had interviewed prior to my relationship falling apart with the intention of having joint income, so the thought of supporting myself on half of what Alina was making scared me. I rarely, if ever, was on time or even slightly late with my rent back home, so I expected nothing less. Fear doesn't seem to affect me like others. I enjoyed the being a fugitive of my consequences. Sober life had less appeal than drinking, but was way more sustainable.

My new boss and all my colleagues, other than a Chinese Singaporean accountant and his Malay Singaporean assistant were French. Despite knowing that I didn't speak a lick of French the owner and upper management continued to speak only French at meetings. They spoke perfect English. The owner of the company, who was French, was asking the general manager about me and motioning her to give me some information as I sat quietly and uselessly at my new desk on my first day.... my French was awful, but I was able to pick up on bits and pieces. I was pretty clever when it came to learning new languages. I actually had been six credits shy of acquiring my Associates degree in culinary arts prior to moving, but tested out of Spanish 101 and Spanish 102 with fluency to earn the credits in a three hour proctored oral examination some weeks before getting to Singapore. Good thing, too, because degrees are required to obtain international working visas. Most of language was unspoken, anyway. Maybe out of context alone, I presumed I could figure most things out. Either way, I moved past the language barrier with earnest. The owner, Michel, seemed fond of me. The company was spread throughout six SE Asian countries and one man pulled all the strings. I thought... what an awesome life this guy must have. I was thirsty for adventure. His purpose in beckoning the GM towards me was to instruct me on my objective with them. It was my first day on the job, and in spite of his outward language disrespectfulness, he was hopeful of my success in Singapore and truly cared that his people have all the resources they need to succeed. He had the general manager, Cari, hand me a piece of graph paper out of her notebook and told her to explain the way he wanted his kitchen laid out to me. I had never designed anything other than a twelve-inch plate full of food.

She explained, "Each square represents a twenty-five to one size to scale versus reality." She handed me the invoice of kitchen equipment that had been ordered from China months before I was hired. I was off and running. I was hired to lead a kitchen and staff it, cook in it, order for it, and now design it, apparently. I walked my ass down to the site and began developing thoughts. Finally, I thought to myself, I can do new things with wider boundaries with trust as a professional. I used that one sheet of graph paper and designed my first fully functional kitchen. They trusted me without me first offering them trust, and, for that, I was grateful.

Poh, our wine deliveryman, would come in and out of the office between his deliveries around the country. Sounds weird, but Singapore could be lapped several times by car throughout any day. He would chat and ask questions about how I enjoyed Singapore thus far and what I enjoyed doing in my free time. He came in one Friday afternoon with a wry smile on his face. I felt like he was up to something the way he looked at me, and he was. He approached me, leaned over at my desk as I was busy drawing my egresses and water runoffs into my graph sheet.… "You want to go get a girl in Geylang later?" Poh asked. Sometimes I felt like I had mischief written on my face. He offered me the scandalous adventures I gravitated towards in the one place in Singapore you could find trouble. It was implicit of getting a hooker, I thought. I balked at the comment, but I accepted his invite. I was nervous as hell trying to figure out how and why a friendly, physically fit Asian man was inviting me out for pussy when it didn't appear he had much need to be paying for it. I certainly felt as though I could do fine without paying for it, but I was so curious! Poh looked too straight-edge to be involved in what I thought to be seedy activities. Little did I know then it was what everyone there did. It's what every guy did, at least. Poh came to pick me up in the company van at my soon-to-be ex's apartment around seven that night. I was nervous, but I handled myself ok. Poh, as it turned out, knew exactly what he was doing, so I followed his lead. The districts of the Singaporean prostitution blocks offered a tour of whatever sexual reality I wanted to exist in, as long as it was vanilla. Singapore is overly vanilla.

The area we went to is known as Geylang, as I alluded to. I would find out later that night Geylang was a government monitored prostitution area in Singapore that offered a hooker-of-every-color, so to speak. Each block was an assortment of ethnically diverse prostitutes brought in by traffickers to ease the struggles of sexual release from the wound-up Navy boys, in and out of Singapore's bustling ports. Geylang is also the home of Singaporean chili crab; something every human needs to experience at some point in their life. Chef Bourdain later went on to film several shows there, citing Singaporean chili crab as one of his most enjoyable experiences. I would always just chuckle under my breath at the use of the word "experience" as opposed to "meal." The benefit and irony in getting the best crabs in the world in Geylang will always make me chuckle a bit, too, but it's true. Not like that...sick fucks. Poh, my new friend, was thoroughly enjoying my moral conflict the entire time. It wasn't easy to hide my nerves or sweaty palms. That was the night I cracked on my sobriety streak and got an ice-cold beer to ease my nerves. Three years....sayonara.

I digress. I went with the Vietnamese horse that night. She was cute and wearing a short, shiny, silver dress with black heels and loop earrings. She, like the other girls trying to make a few bucks, nodded and half smiled to draw my attention. She was less vocal than the desperate girls. I liked that. We had sex in an hourly room after discussing and agreeing on a price. One hundred and fifty Singapore dollars it was - those were both firsts too. I later spoke to my buddy, Ivas, back home and he asked me if her pussy was sideways. I didn't get it, but I didn't see it. This was the moment I realized the level of ignorance I maintained back in my Boston-based bubble. Her pussy was super hairy, I told him...and I wasn't going down on a hoe...yet. Her lips were insatiably plush and plump, and I felt relieved about the language barrier for the first time in my life because I didn't want the taxi man that Poh dropped us at to know what we were discussing....as if he didn't know! I also detest small talk. I was appreciating the language barrier. She was very sweet and seemingly innocent otherwise. Her name was Jin. I still haven't seen a sideways pussy, and I've seen over three thousand. I'll hold this info from Evelyn and categorically deny ever writing it until she's at least fifteen.

I took the subway everywhere in Singapore, which was a monorail system. It looked clean enough to eat off the floor in

Singaporean subways. Riding it required a card from the ministry of manpower, a government office that mandates employment quotas, taxes, and most other government functions. They were a government watchdog, and that made me slightly uncomfortable. Not uncomfortable enough to walk or pay for taxis, however. The Republic of Singapore has zero crime, and I can't recall ever witnessing anything close to one. Even the wildlife is regulated down to non-harmful species only. Vanilla, vanilla, extra vanilla. Tickets and fines were issued for chewing gum and smoking cigarettes outdoors. I remember being appalled at getting one myself. For someone like me, it's usually better not to try to prove things that had a history of repeating themselves as irrelevant and dismiss them as "old behaviors." My history as an addicted hypo-maniac is and was relevant and would remain relevant as much as I hoped it wouldn't be. I wasn't prepared for the exhausting heat that never went away, even when the sun did. I was starting to think Singapore would be but a brief escape in my journey through life and started to think about moving back to the States.

The work hours got long. My trips to work had me soaked with sweat under the ninety-degree gaze of the sun. I began to spend extra minutes at the Indian temple just outside my office in the morning. I would ask questions. When I didn't want to know the answer, I would just presume things that entertained my questions. That suited me. It still does. After work I would sit at the twenty-four-hour coffee shop, which served anything but coffee, and order sweet and sour pork, watch some soccer, depress my thoughts and adrenaline, and try to get a few hours' sleep.

I had little money and was starting to look for roommates that could put up with me. This shouldn't be hard, I pondered. I justified my insane schedule and steady income and put an ad in the classifieds. My soon-to-be ex-girlfriend had fulfilled my prophecy and was now the latter part of 'soon-to-be-ex'. Easy out call when my search history on her laptop came up with an Asian dating website and unlocked several conversations I preferred she hadn't seen. The outcome was inevitable. I met Lauren through the ads I had posted. Lauren would be a hard to follow, hardworking, Australian girl that had some boring job, but she was cool, and I didn't want to fuck her. That helped me feel better about my potential home situation. We decided to pool our resources and look at flats. We found one in no time sitting above a restaurant. It was a three-bedroom unit, however, and twenty minutes outside the CBD, or central business district. We put another ad out to fill that third bedroom and met Greg, an American…. a cohort. Greg was a cool guy. E-commerce something or other. He was a riot, and we all laughed and shared stories. We also shared a similar sense of humor, which is nearly impossible to find in Asia. Sarcasm is taken as literal, which would benefit my personality to no end while I was there. Kind of ironic and funny.

We brought in Greg, and life was manageable…at least, that's what I thought. As things moved along in Singapore, I realized how unmanageable my salary versus the cost of living was. I was drowning in mediocrity and exhaustion, and there was only so many French nationals I could stand on a daily basis. I got myself a Citibank credit card with a five-thousand-dollar limit. I thought about how to blow it, and it didn't take long. I booked a ticket to Bangkok. I went for the weekend warrior pass, and I crushed it. I remember looking for girls and cocaine, which seemed to be the easiest two things to find in Bangkok. By this point in life, I had never even heard of methamphetamines. My addictions had been to everything else up until then. I found what I was looking for that weekend in abundance. As the years go on and my story unfolds, you'll agree that you can always find what you're looking for in Bangkok. Keep your wishes simple and safe. After my trip, and having had one to Phuket, Thailand with that ex I spoke of some months before - my new purpose was to move to Thailand. It was a notion I never thought would take on the life it did, but it did.

I responded to an ad by an international consultant that was looking for a chef for a "high profile" beach club in Koh Samui. With my attached resume I included the personal details of my exhaustion and boredom in the sterile streets of Singapore and the fallout with Alina. I still don't know why I added that part- probably the exhaustion of the schedule I was locked into. Funny thing about it, I was the only person he contacted of the over fifteen hundred CVs he received. His name was Jeffrey, and we would go on to find out we thought and spoke a lot alike. We viewed and appreciated our food as approachable above everything. Food was everything until Evelyn came along. I would never have anticipated anything trumping my love for food and kitchens up until that point. Anything coming between me and my kitchens was laughable….then.

3 | MALAYSIA – JANUARY 2010

Niki and I had two dogs, one cocker spaniel named T-be and one puppy of T-be's that was born while we lived together, Brownie. We waffled on which of the five puppies to keep, but Brownie kept us. She made me her choice and I returned her love. She was my little floppy-eared soldier. I always had dogs. My dogs will be named and discussed with more value and credited with more influence and happiness in my story than most humans, almost as if they are human, because their impact was usually more memorable than most. That's because of their abilities to discern my emotions and act accordingly with unflinching loyalty. Their innate ability to change the status of my day, and their willingness to be teachable. They are more "people" than my sister-in-law will ever be. Brownie was my sidepiece, literally. She would stick near and fend off any street dogs that wandered too close to me. She was well trained, well behaved, and so affectionate. She loved me and I loved Brownie right back. We later re-homed T-be with Niki's mom, who detested the site of my face or sound of my motorbike. I had gotten a reputation in Koh Samui, and Niki's mom, being so tied to the Thai mafia, was well aware of my whereabouts at all times.

As I started to feel a watchful eye on me, I felt relieved that the island had grown slow with the world recession and things looked dismal from the tourist forecast. Salaries were down and tourism ultimately crept to a slow crawl by the end of 2009. The only people coming were the backpackers resolved to spend their savings and live in the Muay Thai gyms as long as they could until it was time to go back home. Wherever that was. The best or most valuable thing I can add to that is that they weren't American. The lack of job security and projected falloff for the world economy was just the out I was looking for. Koh Samui, or any island for that matter, tends to get smaller and smaller as the days turn over. The honeymoon and fifteen minutes of fame, for me, was over, and I began to feel common and discontented by familiarity.

That was just until my former employer from Singapore reached out explaining they had just launched Bangkok's busiest new restaurant, and they needed me. They were getting pummeled, and I was the devil they knew. They didn't know that 'devil' was a fitting word. I had been mired in the cyclical nightmare that drugs created for me. Meth had been a running constant in my life, and running my life for the last few months I lived in Koh Samui. Fortunately for me, as any foreigner starting a new job in Thailand, I was required to leave the country for a non-B working visa. This was a common trip, and tour vans would assist in the process. It's almost as if the government preemptively struck the chord I was looking for before starting any new role. A chance to start working on a fresh day off of the opportunity to have released any impending resentments or bad habits my last endeavor may have prompted. I was typically clamoring weeks into the job about being overworked, underpaid, and in need of a holiday, something I think most of us that strive for adulthood can attest to. I never had the luxury of time off, because my addiction required me to earn money to feed him.

I chose to go to Penang, Malaysia and spend the weekend at the Banana Inn and reset my life, so I thought, before heading to Bangkok to start my new venture. The Banana Inn is a well-known hotspot for tourists hell-bent and dead set on getting that last hurrah before starting a new job and tearing it up in a little relatively unknown town in northern Malaysia. What happens in Penang stays in Penang!

Niki and I talked about resetting our relationship as well. She wanted to come, so I agreed. We packed a backpack apiece and met the van at four in the morning at the pier in Nathon, Koh Samui. The next few days would be an unnecessary challenge to everything I knew about crossing borders and the corrupt systems that handled the process.

There were six of us plus the driver in the van. One American guy that worked as a scuba dive instructor in Koh Tao, a small diver's island north of Koh Samui accessible only by boats, two British girls that seemed appalled that I was bringing a Thai national on an expat's journey, Niki, a Canadian idiot named Curtis Apache, and myself.

I recall being at peace with the thought of rejoining my former employer and trying to rediscover the passion that had been fading between Niki and I. The cosmic gods, unfortunately, had different plans for us. The trip, boring and listless, spanned through the southern peninsula of Thailand into Sadao, the southernmost point of Thailand. The countryside was desolate. I recall driving through endless rubber tree farms. They were beautiful in terms of symmetry, yet as distinctively short in character as the next. More so, even, was their lack of and shape and distinction from one to the next - maze-like but easily navigated. Rows of leafless trunks were systematically planted to provide the rubber farmers enough distance to tap into and enough silence to even hear the rubber sap pour. It was pretty its simplicity. I remember the rubber tree farm fighting scene from Mortal Kombat where the two ninjas, Scorpion and Subzero, flexed their superpowers in the first movie attempt at recreating the video game onto the big screen. That's where I recognized rubber trees from. Most of my knowledge comes from an inexplicable ability to capture and retain my memories in a photogenic way. Movies and experience, that's my source.

The van was now getting close to the border. The driver had given the rest of us the nod to start prepping our belongings for inspection as well as our documents for immigration control as we approached

Sadao. Sadao was a strange place. Not quite Thailand and not quite Malaysia. It's the border town and belongs to Thailand, yet it is equally populated by Malaysians on foot. The Malaysian men would sneak up to the border and abscond across for a night, a week, a lifetime of pleasure and sexual fulfillment away from the ambivalence that is Malaysian culture. The black…no, eggplant-colored men lurk awkwardly in the streets searching for a willing trick, eager to not appear too eager. Hoping for eye contact from a desperate girl in need of money and willing to compromise her integrity and standards. The men were not bad men, but they had no game, no looks, no money, and to add that all up, they had even less hope of fulfilling their desires. But they persisted. Some succeeded, actually. I felt bad for the girls. See, prostitution isn't legal in Thailand, but there are pussy poles and bright lights in every seedy corner of the country, flaunting the beauty of their women and culture and land. Malaysia was so different, and the men realized this. Thailand was beautiful. Thailand is beautiful.

As we approached the border Niki and I prepared our passports and bags for search. We were excited to get to the inn, which was about ninety minutes over the border and cast our rods of relaxation in a one-star rathole. The point was just to be together, awaiting confirmation in the form of a three-by-four-inch sticker affixed to the next available spot of my passport that read "non-B working visa." It was a confirmed symbol of our next journey and one year extension to my already established and blossoming career. Our bags and intentions were clean and pure.

While I was getting eye-fucked by immigration officers, they seemed to take notice of Niki. It was hard not to. If her looks didn't get you, then her slick mouth certainly would. The purpose of their interest was soon to be unveiled. I did mention I had an intimidating build. I took shit from no one, but the thought of adding contention to three armed guards with unstrapped automatic rifles was not a battle I wanted to provoke. I remained quiet. The six of us and the driver were eschewed to the rear of the vehicle upon being met at the last checkpoint in our exit process- actually, five of us were. Niki was interrupted in her compliance while walking to the back and rerouted to the immigration office. I began getting curious as to why they wanted her attention. I can't say I blamed them, but I wasn't fond of sharing. I wasn't dumb enough to let them see that. I saw Niki point towards me, and I felt relief. I thought she was telling them what a fucking upstanding guy I was and how we were set to spend a couple days in Penang with the crew awaiting a new visa. Niki being a Thai national mustn't have brought her poker face that day, and compound that with a matter-of-fact tone and the fact that it was her time of the month, must have forgotten my life was waiting in the balance of her remark. She was telling them that I was decent and working in the Kingdom of Thailand as a chef, but the officers decided to go with their skepticisms and pull me to the ground in a violent takedown from behind.... as two officers stood over me aiming rifles toward my noggin. I was scared, disturbed, and suddenly in fear of my life. "That bitch!" I thought. "Double-crossing cunt!"

Niki was still just seventeen, and after being dragged away without my bag or my belongings by my armpits into the back door of the immigration office with the most intimidating of the officers intently following my legs in tow, I found out that Niki was now being escorted out. She yelled, "Matt, they think you're fucking human trafficking!" This all made sense now. How naive must I have been? Don't answer that…it would be too easy. The thing about human trafficking is it isn't something easy to prove without admission from the victimized party. Apparently, Niki's mom had made a few calls before we arrived at the border. They were waiting for me. Niki didn't confirm nor deny our purpose in Penang, thus, making it a conundrum for immigration control. I remember looking out the window of the back office and seeing my tour van disappear into the landscape of the Malaysian border. I felt deflated…utterly flat. I was lost, scared, anxious, and unequivocally defeated. I had no money or means to survive in Sadao and the thought of another minute in the town would have been one longer than I ever wanted to spend there again. I was stuck, but I still had my passport.

After a couple hours of sitting isolated in the room I was brought to the checkpoint to proceed over the border. I was feeling better. Thais don't negotiate with foreigners nor do they interrogate them. They simply take you or leave you. I was awaiting getting pole-axed and thrown in the Bangkok Hilton or even worse, a southern Thai prison and forgotten. So, progress towards the resolution, or intended resolution, was awesome! All I needed was my stamp to pass the test. It looked like their research proved that I was an innocent, well...for all intents and purposes as it relates to human trafficking. The immigration officer glanced at my passport as it appeared I would be free - still lost and stranded, but free. That was more than I could have said minutes before. The officer adamantly explained in Thai that the stamp I had from Koh Samui was not valid in his office (legally it was) and if I wanted to get over the border, I would pay him twenty thousand baht, minimum. Extortion at its finest. I had heard about this in Thailand and experienced it on a much more pedestrian and G-rated scale later on, but I never thought I would be a victim of it. I use the word victim, but it's clear at this point of my story that I am anything but. I was thirty-one years old traveling with and insatiably gorgeous seventeen-year-old Thai girl. I was an idiot! Had the extortion amount been in dollars I would have called it a day and asked for a quiet cell. Niki had convinced them I was innocent, so their next chink in the chain was to prevent my passage, or at least my safe passage. I had no money, which seemed to infuriate the officer more. White men in Thailand are expected to pay when asked - it's that simple. I did what any broke wise man would do. I turned and walked back towards Sadao in hopes of disappearing beyond the gaze of the immigration office. I felt relief as I drifted out of sight, but I recall hearing the officer tell another officer that I wasn't going to Malaysia without that money.

Sadao, to my surprise, actually had one Western Union. I got there minutes before closing as the sun was now beginning to set on the day and my hope. I found an Internet cafe and emailed my parents in desperation. I spared them the trafficking details, but thankfully they didn't insist in their reply on having them. I received the MTCN, the only way to collect a wire transfer, from my amazing parents. We'll touch on them a bit later. I wasn't always so amazing to them, but they were always my standard for human integrity for as long as I could remember. I remember everything, remember?

The money office of Western Union was closed, and the night fell. I found a seedy avenue, and another, which always seemed to find me more often than I found them and began to search for a hotel that would accept a printed copy of the email from my parents with the MTCN (two numbers blacked out, of course) to assure they would receive payment the next morning. I went from alley to alley like Will Smith in I Am Legend awaiting the night crawlers in the absence of sunlight. I found a taker. It was the first time I could communicate outwardly in Thai language and complete a transaction without English. The front office staff spoke no English. It's amazing where desperation brings the human mind. To this point my Thai lessons were those from bargirls I got head from, and it's pretty difficult getting the full lesson when the language teacher has a mouth full of phallic manhood. Ew, I know, but true. I was told when I got to Thailand that it was hard to learn - most foreigners I knew spoke little to no Thai because of its difficulty to learn - going from a Germanic, Latin based language to one that is communicated through monosyllabic tones ranging from high, ascending, descending, low, and middle. Painful at times and humiliating the rest, but I insisted on learning. I was proud of myself, nonetheless. Evelyn's first language was Thai, but she speaks very little now. Shameful from a parent's perspective, but the mind dismisses what it doesn't get interest or stimulation from. She's American through and through and fucking proud to be…more so than I. My distaste in my own indigenous culture grows by the day. It's as if we are regressive in our evolution and living as if it's ok to treat people based on our presumptions. Americans naturally cannot answer a direct question. Our answers are typically predicated on our presumed notion to what your question implies as if we are speeding along the conversation by doing so, where in fact, we sound like pedantic pontificating clowns. No real qualifications or clairvoyance, just ignorance. I digress.

As the sun split the land and sky overlooking the eastern peninsula the next morning, I started to motivate myself and prayed for the courage, patience, and fortitude to get myself to Penang. My non-B visa and future employment were now my primal and growing concern. I had been released from custody by the immigration office and given the bounty for my intrusion into their world, as they saw it. The only thing left was to procure the money for my safe passage into Malaysia. Niki, as far as I knew, was lounging at the Banana Inn with the rest of the crew enjoying a Leo beer and spending my money without reservation. It was ok, money is just money, and I never really cared too much about it, so long as I had enough to get by. At that time in 2010, the sole Western Union in this seedy, bizarro world of Sadao was my only hope. When I added in the unprovoked prejudice of the immigration office, this was going to add anxiety from projecting the unknown to this already high stress situation. The outcome of my days work would ultimately be the difference in my status as a resident of the Kingdom and potentially jeopardize being black stamped. Something the Tao specifically warns against is projecting and placing the mind in any outcome or turmoil that isn't our present moment of existence. Moment to moment, the only thing we as humans are expected to devote our attention to is the 'here and now'. The present, because the 'now' is the only situation we have the opportunity to live in and effect. I waffle on the word "control" because there is no such thing. I get that…it took a while, but I get it. Moment by moment, we pave the path to success by making good decisions in succession, which molds our perception of control; however, it is only a façade.

As I sit on the steps with the front office staff of the hotel awaiting a motorbike taxi that will take us both to Western Union to ensure my promise is kept, I search through my pockets and dig out the email and my passport. I was off with the taxi.

Once I collected the money, the hotel staff, being appreciative of my congruence, asked the taxi man to continue my trip onto the border. Perplexed at why a foreigner is walking alone into Malaysia without transportation other than my own two feet with miles of road ahead of me, he collects his fare and speeds away. Had I known the word for passport in Thai, I would have asked him to accompany me into the first inhabited town once over the border, but this was not a conversation I needed to have just yet. First was getting my alleged overstay paid and clearing the illegal stamp I was supposedly carrying naively in my passport full of dulled, overworked ink.

As I entered the office the staff greeted me and seemed to not know or remember who I was. My officer friends from the night before weren't there, so I explained my situation in simple, toddler-worthy English to the first immigration officer with an open turnstile. He asked me to hold while another office made sure I didn't try to cross or run. Minutes later he came back with a confused look on his face and said he had no idea what I was talking about, but my stamp was valid and my exit from the Kingdom was as easy as walking myself over the border. I was adulated, although I didn't show it. I confidently went through the turnstile and slipped past with a thank you in Thai, and I was officially funded and free. I could now figure out my transportation and get into Penang, and I did.

As I pulled up to the Banana Inn my entire crew was hooting and clapping and seemingly drunk. No...definitely drunk. They had been so worried. Niki was just walking out from what was expectedly a long night of fear in solitude in a new city without contact with anyone other than our drunken cohorts. The look of relied on her face as I jumped out of a coconut truck driven by a kind Malay was authentic. We now had a Malaysian fortune as I still had the ransom money, and we all knew we were about to have a great couple of days full of stories and ephemeral bonds made with our new comrades, me being the triumphant prodigal son with cash to boot and the means to all our ends.

Life felt good. Life was good, in that moment. We partied. The Canadian, Curtis Apache, and I shared stories. He was a journey fisherman who shared pictures and tales of river monsters and drunkenness. We found meth and hid in an extra room that we rented for the sole purpose of getting high and anticipatory prostitutes. Niki would be passed out by now, and the day wasn't even old enough to be dusk. Niki never approved of drugs, so her being a lightweight that day was all too convenient. I never felt any kind of guilt in the poor decisions I made while high, not until I straightened out for long enough for my soul to re-enter my body. That was a perfect way to describe what methamphetamines did to someone - they burned your soul right out of your body. Mine was on hiatus as we took hit after hit off a foil ribbon we tore off the roll we bought at the inn's toiletry vending machine. Another resourceful tool I inherited while in Asia, not that an addict ever needs lessons to find a way to ingest their substances. You can rest assured that no addict is giving in to lack of options in how they use with a pocketful of their substance of choice. Most would laugh at even the mention of such crap. We got high, Curtis and I, and we found all the trouble we were looking for. By this time the thought of my new job, Niki, the dogs, and life in general were all relegated to priority number two.

Methamphetamine was the winner as I look back, partly with shame and guilt, and I would take the newly found love-of-my-life and all the misery it would bring with it to Bangkok in the coming days to start our new perverse and utopian lives together…at least while we were together.

The streets of Bangkok are widely known for fresh food stalls, lady-boys, and traffic. It was time to move on to Bangkok – me, Niki, Brownie, Herbie, and Lola. Herbie and Lola were to two most beautiful yet spiteful beagles in existence, but they were family. They were loved. My decision was clear, but Niki waffled. She would take some time to think about the move with her mother's incessant warnings about my shenanigans on the island. Her mother was right, but Niki came anyway….at least on and off at my expense.

4 | BANGKOK - 2010

It's tough to shake the first impression of any known noun when it hits you in a way that no other place ever has, even when it is pinned almost exactly on the map opposite my place of birth, which is Lawrence, Massachusetts. My mother would always joke that if I kept digging up mud-meatballs and filling my wheelbarrow with dirt from the same hole... that I would end up popping out somewhere in China. She was close. I would have surfaced in Bangkok. Little did I know then it would have been perfectly fine from my current stance. Bangkok, or Krung Thep to the Thais, was my city - a place that everything felt instantaneously comfortable. I still consider Bangkok my true home, and after having lived in a perpetually changing set of walls on new soil with new government, I can unflinchingly assess Bangkok as the city I knew and loved most. It is my place of sanctity and comfort. I can handle myself pretty well, and by this point my Thai was adequate enough to fit right into conversations regardless of the context. Having been in an addicted hell through the latter days of my time in Koh Samui, I was determined to shake off the half measures in efforts of remaining sober I had put forth thus far and solidify myself as a legitimate chef in the city that was named world's greatest in 2010. Addiction, however, when swamped in its desolation, has a different plan for us, unfortunately. There's something about the twenty-four-hour availability of just about anything a human could conjure up with amazingly simple people so willing to provide you happiness, time, and attention that makes the land and culture buoyantly appealing.

I arrived early 2010 with my three dogs in tow on a train while Niki remained back in Koh Samui. I needed and appreciated the space. However, it was space that provided loneliness and defeat as my work hours grew long and my dogs suffered their own destitute path. I was up at five in the morning and home at ten at night and managed to sneak away for a couple jaunts back to my studio apartment to get the dogs some outdoor play during the days. I was exhausted. They were getting spiteful, as beagles tend to do, but Brownie was always understanding of my new role. I could always tell her level of understanding through her big brown eyes. They spoke volumes. As time went on, the beagles, who were too erratic in their behavior to be trusted, would stay home while Brownie trailed me to work and sat at the back door of the restaurant. She survived off scraps offered by the staff while they were cleaning meats and vegetables. She took a few minutes to share a meal with me just before I whisked myself off in a hurry to tend to the next fire that needed smoldering. This was typically the chosen path and only path I've ever known - it has been and always will be in a chef's world. There are no hours off to chefs. We, or I, so as to not group the healthy chefs in my attempt at self-validation through my failing career, had this insane thought that what I did was so important it warranted giving away every potentially notable day in my life. Weddings, holidays, and birthdays were unimportant, and time off, never mind days off, was unwanted. I acted as if my job were to cure cancer or save mankind when I couldn't even save myself. I was just sick. Mentally and physically polluted. Brownie stuck by my side, however, sick or not.

As was the case in most of my new roles, I made immediate enhancements to the operation. Our unit was getting pummeled from a business standpoint; doors were lined with Thais waiting to get through the glass door that wrapped around restaurant in the newest Bangkok hotspot. People came to see the magnificent charcuterie and fromagerie cases and sip on imported wines while being noticed and posting to their social medias about how they actually made it through the WTA doors. WTA was the business acronym for my Singaporean based employer, now killing it in Bangkok. We served royalty and celebrities, common people and foreigners who couldn't stomach Thai food. WTA was for everyone. The lot outside was typically spaced with Aston Martins, Rolls Royce, Teslas, and Bentleys. Thais knew how to flaunt their wealth, and WTA was quickly becoming the best and most noticeable venue to do so.

My apartment was a quick five-minute drive, and in between my apartment and work was the infamous Nana Square. Driving through Nana at any time of the day was an adventure. Nana, during daylight, was host to tourists, full service massage parlors, prostitutes, pubs, street food vendors, and a range of hotels of various star ratings, from five-star dream suites to some I'm not sure were worthy of the one they claimed having. As night fell, the men from African cartels filled the alleys in Nana awaiting eye contact from strangers to let them know it was ok to pedal whatever drug they were carrying my way. Prostitutes and lady-boys aggressively reached out for a white skinned arm in desperation for a trick, bellowing for the chance to give blowjobs for short money. Street hawkers set up bootlegged DVD stalls, tables flipped out of vans with Cialis, Viagra, meth pipes, blow torches, and whatever else attracted the seedy sub-culture, tuk-tuks, taxis, and motorbikes awaited foot traffic to throw up an arm and summon them so they could retire the overexposed bodies back to whatever seedy hole they crawled out of. Nana was always bumper-to-bumper with traffic no matter the hour. This lifestyle seemed to attract the least attractive souls on any corner of the globe. Nana was a place where no one had a name, and most people didn't use their real one anyway. Police could also be found in abundance in Nana, but they weren't upholding the law. Protect and serve meant shaking money from the pockets of foreign prostitutes in order to protect and serve their financial status. I would catch ear of Russian hookers pleading in alleyways to have more time. They obviously had spent the officer's ransom on drugs, so the officer seemed upset. Shakedowns like this were common, and I laughed out loud to the point of drawing attention to myself at times. It wasn't funny, but having white privilege and a steady job gave me the false impression that I was invincible. I certainly am not.

African men would be seen rallying in protest at any hour when one of their brothers in drug pedaling arms was executed for wandering too far off the path of the turned eye. African men were allowed to be on Soi 3 and stayed unbothered there, but when a sale took them a street or two over, police then enforced martial law and would shoot to kill. These men were sent to the Thai version of a morgue and gutted to reduce body weight, packed in a cardboard box, and shipped back to their country at a reasonable cost. It is rumored the governments of these African nations and the Thai government have an agreement that this is standard procedure. As I hear, the opportunity to leave Nigeria, Zambia, Cameroon, Congo, and others is so appealing, even without a passport, that slinging drugs by swallowing a pack of narcotics wrapped in electrical tape is actually considered an opportunity. Yeah, Nana was that bad. The beauty of everything I knew Thailand to be was starting to fade, not because it didn't stay intact, but because I couldn't stay intact. Mentally and physically, my need for meth was taking me to Nana Square on a nightly basis. I was addicted to everything about the drug and the scene. I was polluted from the inside out. My weight was down, anxiety was through the roof, and my hours of sleep in any given week could have been counted on one hand. I started most dusks at Soi 3 looking for my dealer after work, and often before I should have left work. From there I found a taxi to my room. Most addicts can attest to the self-driven anxiety of having your high in your pocket and being stuck in traffic or in a place where using was impossible and getting so anxious the thought of using became so panicked that risking imprisonment or death seemed like a valid option. I was no different. I usually maintained my composure, as difficult as it was...usually. I recall being less than three hundred meters from my hotel room and ducking into an alleyway to catch a hit off the meth-laced foil I had scrunched up in my pocket so I could be in top notch form for the girl I had waiting for me. I also would prefer to say I had less drugs than I did and smoking some before I got there made that an honest statement. As a sober human I would give my last twenty dollars to anyone that I felt needed it more than I did. In my active addiction I would steal your purse or rifle through your wallet, take money out, and photograph your credit cards to use for online shopping or cash advances. As I exited the alley, I was met by two officers on a single motorbike. They jumped off and darted towards me. I was fucked.

I heard of a kid in Koh Samui whose girlfriend planted yabba (pills cooked with meth and heroin), a Thai speedball, in his bungalow, and called police. Darren, the kid I'm referring to, was thrown in the Bangkok Hilton, a prison where up to twelve men share a six-by-six cell and are essentially forgotten by the world. This was all I could think of as the cops surrounded me while I crumpled up the foil as discreetly as I could. My passport was in my pocket, but it was a mess. My allotted time, by this point, to recover the pages I lost in futile arguments by bar girls I shorted on sex payment was given freely and most necessarily to the streets of Nana, as my addiction justified, was now lost. The cops pulled my arms from each side and grabbed my hands to pry them open.... the foil fell out. As one officer restrained me and the other slowly unwrapped the foil - all I could think about was my tomorrow. Would I have one? I reckoned not. Fate, be it a twisted bitch, was on my side that night. The officer looked perplexedly into the foil wrapper and saw nothing. Meth has a way in its crystallized form of appearing invisible in certain lights. The light was in my favor and the officer discarded it as a candy wrapper. My explanation was sound, but that didn't excuse the small bag of meth that I had just tucked in my pocket, or so I thought, before leaving the alley. As the officers now spun me towards the wall and began to search my pockets, I heard one say to the other, "Mai mee arai." That was nothing short of miraculous. It wouldn't be the first time I mistakenly forgot my drugs behind, but this was the most notable and fortunate of those scenarios. The bag of meth was left in the alley. I was free. Free from the persecution of the Thai judicial system, but not from my addiction. Honestly, even after hearing the fate or potential fate of having been caught with drugs, I still prefer that of the Thai courts.

The days at work grew shorter and shorter. My team was now

spread out through overnight shifts because we were unable to accommodate the guests with our output during normal operating hours as sales grew to inconceivable levels. I was vetting new vendors daily to comply with our business. Day after day I was handed business cards from prospective vendors. I, like most chefs, discarded these as easily as gum wrappers. There was one vendor whom I took particular interest in. She was unannounced and unscheduled...the least welcome type of vendor meetings. Impromptu. The hostess, Apple, came to fetch me in the kitchen, but I graciously declined as the kitchen was taxed with orders and drama. Apple insisted I make the most of my vendor meetings as to not get a bad reputation in Bangkok. I obliged. As I turned the corner around the cheese displays, past the wine room, and into the dining room I saw, sitting alone, a chipmunk-cheeked cutie in a short, gray, wool, button-up dress. She had long, straight, brown hair pulled back to depict her businesslike intentions.

Her name, as we exchanged introductions, was Annie. She is still the devil emoji with the upside-down smile and always will be, but she wasn't that day. That day she was my next target. She was bashful and noticeably new at her job making her vulnerable and all the more exposed to a sexual deviant like myself. Men like me thrived on vulnerability. She was pitching her product with brochures and pricing guides while I inspected her facial contours and gawked at her perky breasts and slim waist in her little button-down dress. Annie reached just over five feet in height and was about ninety pounds, about the size of most petite Thai women. I had a thing for petite and cute. What guy doesn't, really? She could tell I was in a bit of rush, however, and as I was about to interrupt her mid-pitch, she mindfully called attention to my busy schedule (or the impending look of dismissal on my face) and offered to wrap up her seafood spiel in a "just a moment." She may have also noticed the only seafood on our menu was shrimp that accompanied a pasta dish. She seemed more confident the less she talked about product and the more she bantered. Her smile was infectious. She briefly opened up to talk about her schedule and her mother back home. She smiled a lot. I couldn't help but notice.

As she tucked her seafood pamphlets into her notebook and went to pack them in her bag to prepare herself for her next spiel with the next impatient chef, she asked where I was living and how I was enjoying Bangkok. I kept my answers short, knowing this gives girls the impression that I'm not interested, making it more (if ever) necessary to capture some attention. It's as if women enjoyed being dismissed. It makes them frantically insistent on getting the attention they were so accustomed to from most other men. I prided myself on never being like most other men, and furthermore, I found most girls won't seek a decent man until enough deplorable men have gone unfazed by their futile attempts to change them or, at the very least, change how they act and feel towards them, making them the sole survivor in the revolving pool of women us dickhead-ish characters engage with romantically through their lives. Annie was looking for a guy to take care of. It was now clear, as she continued to seek a common interest, that I was her target, as well. As I went on about the stress and blabbered about my favorite topic, myself, I saw her perked for an interjection. How the tides were turned. I was explaining the dogs back home in my studio and how important it was for me to get home a couple times throughout the day to take them outside. The next words poised on her lips would change the life I lived and my entire life henceforth forever. "I would love to help you take the dogs out. I love dogs," Annie replied.

As the next week unfolded, I realized Annie was not only going to walk the dogs at my apartment, free of charge, but she would bring a few groceries and clean up my disheveled apartment. She even brushed my meth pipes and placed my empty baggies into a drawer for my privacy. Her efforts were clearly aimed at partnering up in life with me, or was I taking it too far? I had the propensity to do that, too. I found it odd that she didn't scoff or balk at or even mention the paraphernalia, but she was also very inexperienced in life and probably didn't want to bring it up. Maybe she didn't understand it's purpose. Either way, my addiction was elated at this notion.

My next curiosity, or growing skepticism, was why she wanted to play any role in the life if a man who lives at work, offers little attention, and clearly is awaiting, as you recall, the return of his girlfriend from Koh Samui. Not to mention an obvious raging drug habit. Niki had been growing more and more anxious to come back to me, and the less I engaged with her, the more desperate she was to rejoin me. As my awkward and tension-filled relationship with

Annie unfolded I explained that her volunteer duties would soon be expiring as Niki was coming back. We had been only platonic until this point. Despite Annie's obvious feelings, I had a growing discomfort in her presence and an unwillingness to take advantage of the cute girl that was posturing for seafood sales a few days back. The target was lifted and refocused. Something I never thought to move on from until I had at least had sex with someone. It was very weird...but she was weird too. Nonetheless, I found myself days before Niki's arrival catching a moment to jump on a motorbike taxi out the back door of work to try to catch Annie at my apartment before she headed out. My motives were physical only. I completely contradict myself regularly within a twenty-four-hour span. We all need a release, and I was addicted to sex as much as I was addicted to methamphetamines.

We met walking through the door at the same time, and there must have been pheromones in the air that day because Annie voiced immediately, with a line in the proverbial sand, how intent she was on becoming my girlfriend. Every man knows that this player's card entitled them to the lustful conclusion they envisioned, so I kiddingly rejected her initial strike, and my eyes and demeanor prompted her for another as I played the fool. Before the next words were finished leaving her throat, my tongue was in it...we were going at it. Annie, to my surprise, was quite inexperienced and reserved, sexually at least. All that talk and the line in the sand bullshit led us to, for all intents and purposes, a very pedestrian and listless sexual experience. As we got dressed and she gave me a sloppy kiss I pulled my attention back to my work and whisked away in my usual regrettable fashion. It was over. In my mind, I couldn't ever see myself with Annie, but at least now I knew, and that is the moment most men know - the exact moment after release. That is what makes us different species as a whole. Annie was not my girl.

Materialistically, I take care of nothing. It doesn't bother me one bit nor has it ever. I've handed over Ray-Bans to a Jamaican on my Negril spring break simply because he looked better in them than I did and he wanted them. I never thought twice about stuff like that. People-pleasing, as it's domestically called, is also the trait of most addicts. Emotionally, in contrast, I take care of EVERYTHING! This is also a trait of addicts. This being said, after getting back to work and avoiding the texts from Annie that were obvious attempts at fishing for reciprocated feelings about our latest sexual experience, I decided to put an end to the glowing on her end and send her back into her gruelingly monotonous, at best, lifestyle and overall state of blissfully ignorant contentment.

For some reason, maybe it was the drugs and lapse of time associated with sleepless weeks on meth, I waited over a week to let Annie know what I knew and had felt moments after we separated ourselves physically that day. As I woke with intent some days later, ten to be exact, the texts from Annie were just as consistent and well timed as they were the last day we saw each other. The ghosting method was clearly not going to cut it. I opened my flip phone and hit send on the call. Muffling the words we exchanged was the intermittent dead air caused by an incoming call. It was Niki I made the breakup call with Annie as rushed as one could to avoid being questioned even though it had been weeks since we had talked on the phone. I tell myself that was my reasoning in hopes of someday believing my own bullshit. Reality was no one likes to have the difficult conversations. Transparency was a foreign word to me at this stage of life and lies were widely accepted as forms of emotional currency. They were my protection. I was really starting to miss Niki's presence, and vagina, in my life.

Annie was curt and as expecting as anyone would be with someone who pulled a hit and quit on them. I was relieved, temporarily, at hearing Niki's voice on the other end. Annie was a thing of the past, and I could refocus on moving forward. Niki, to my intended surprise, was blocks away stuck in traffic and on her way to me. I had little time and wanted to see her, so I anxiously waited at the gate to give her a warm hug and let her know I would get out as soon as I could and take her out. Niki was pretty excited to be surprising me, knowing I would be excited if things were good and awkward if things were sketchy. It was a double-sided win for her. I saw her for a moment as she flaunted her new nose job as if she found the answers to her life's work as a model and credited her newfound confidence and swagger to the completion, as she saw it. I was happy for her…beyond happy. I was even happier it had all healed over and I wouldn't have to "go easy" later when I got home.

I had an aching to put a hurting on her vagina with a long overdue punch in the pants.

That aching was never fulfilled. Not the way I wanted it to be. As I pulled into work and jumped off my motorbike taxi I saw Annie sitting alone at a table in the rear of the restaurant. Her gaze was intense and she was tapping her feet incessantly while folding and unfolding her hands in the most uncomfortable way. I had pretty good intuition on what she wanted, but that was my ego talking. The real purpose was the seedling of my line that was planted in her belly from that day we shared. That one day turned into the most notable day of my life, and it was mildly awkward at its climax. She was pregnant. My life started that day…. I hurriedly went to tell my GM something came up and asked Annie to confirm this with me by her side at one of Bangkok's best hospitals. We drove in her car over to Samitivej Hospital, the same hospital the king went to, and asked for a blood test. I sat there with a million thoughts and scenarios running through me at the speed of light. The only conclusion I could make was that there was no chance that I would forfeit my rights, biological or otherwise, to being a father. Children were something I dreamed of. The thought of being a father was the first time real fear hit me. There are a range of options I was contemplating. I was sweating. The most logical option in my mind was to try being a faithful partner in hopes of keeping my baby in my life. I had no thoughts of shared parenting or monthly or weekly visitation. I knew I would ultimately return to the States, and the projected feelings of that circumstance were scarier than the thought of being a father. I needed this child and I still do. As Annie came out of the nurses' station with the confirmation of her pregnancy, my white complexion turned even more chalk-like and pale. I have never experienced this feeling again. It was real fear.

We sat uncomfortably in her car afterwards contemplating our future and offering "what-if" scenarios before getting into the real negotiations, which we both agreed was a bit heavy after the long day. Theoretically, anything would suffice as long as it encompassed my fatherhood on a full time, visceral level. We decided to talk again the following day while I would return to my pre-interrupted life and get home. "Shit!" I thought to myself. Niki was at my place!

Returning to my apartment was something I contemplated not even following through with. I weighed every scenario again. Blocking a call in June of 2010 wasn't an option yet. The most appealing was disappearance, as I so notably referenced in originally ghosting Annie, but something else I never felt before curdled my stomach - an inclination towards integrity. Starting the process with some level of purity was important to me. The drive home alone in the taxi that night took particularly long. I had time to gather my thoughts and rehearse my delivery to Niki. The dogs were waiting for me too. I even got out a few blocks early that night to sit with my thoughts on a curb and pray. Prayer for men like me is desperation and usually way too late when we've come to that kind of resolve. There's no undoing a pregnancy. Even if abortion was acceptable in Thailand, I am pro-choice! All the practice in the world can't prepare someone for that news. I tried and I failed. I did address the news with Niki promptly, without small talk. I told her of my intentions to be a father to my unknown, tadpole of a child with the passion I unapologetically felt in as authentic a way as I felt it. I'm sure this took Niki aback more than she let on, but that has been the only level of passion towards fatherhood I know. The only road I know. I was met with the fervor I still maintain to this day in every morsel of my humanity as a dad.

Niki was always a jealous girlfriend and set unrealistic boundaries, so dealing with this news was almost inconceivable. She fell to the floor for dramatic effect. Well played, however, the boundary is clearly shattered when a partner impregnates his dog walker. That was indefensible, so I took the high road and manned up. I offered, to no consolation, a plane back to Koh Samui and enough money to take it easy for a couple weeks. I offered to be a platonic friend going forward. I believe I saw her throw up in her mouth a little, but I understood. What I never came to understand was the pleasure she took in slicing and destroying every known possession I had accumulated, including clothes, couches, art, and electronics. I later heard some of my Thai friends joke that this was "Thai style!" I wasn't the lone foreign expatriate experiencing this pushback, but I was the most naive. Needless to say, Niki helped me reset my material world with a fresh wardrobe, and in the coming days, a new, safe apartment.

My mother always warned me, "Hell hath no fury like a woman scorned." Mothers have an uncanny ability to foresee hardship and fallout, but mine and Niki's let us fail. As necessary as it is, there is still no reprieve from the emotional grievances caused by overstepping boundaries so egregiously. I didn't care anymore. I was going to be a dad! The rest of the world could kiss my ass.

Bangkok was ablaze, riddled with political upheavals and curfew stemming from the anarchy and violent demonstrations from hugely contested riots of third party radicals in July of 2010. The Thai government was falling fast. The king, in his twilight years, unable continue his service to his people, was alone in his attempts to quell the uprisings. The prime minister even forbade being out after ten o'clock at night for consecutive days. The king's son and heir to the throne was reportedly committed to the rioting party, the red shirts. This was an important event in my life, surprisingly. As this was unfolding in front of me in a city I loved, I was conveniently contacted by a headhunter in Manila, Philippines to discuss an opportunity there. I accepted the interview, in light of Bangkok's current political situation, and spoke with the HR director at the hotel I was being recruited for. She spoke about the group as a prestigious and well-established enterprise and went on to explain what interested them in retaining me for their northernmost property, Manila Pavilion. The group was called Waterfront Hotels and Casinos and they were a small group consisting of three four-star properties with a resort and boutique style hotel, one five-star property, and one not worth mentioning. The one not worth mentioning was the Manila Pavilion. This particular hotel was suffering from its geographical affliction. It was centered in a poverty stricken neighborhood in East Manila overlooking the boulevard. I knew very little about the Philippines, but I knew I didn't want to go there for their least profitable hotel. I was flattered, but graciously declined.

Annie was getting into her second trimester and things were holding up with us thus far. We moved in together in a flat about a block from my work so I could be available if need be. Annie still spent enough nights at her mom's place and was naive enough as well as pre-consumed with the pregnancy that I could still use almost every night. I credited my now-overblown addiction to meth on several things, just none of them myself. I blamed the stress in my attention to our unborn baby and my ability to manipulate Annie into whatever role I needed her to play. I still maintain that there was no chance in me ever actually loving Annie. I loved who was in her belly while I practiced restraint and acceptance in my relationship. I was rotting from the inside, and I took it out on Annie. I was in Nana Square almost every night, getting high and picking up a girl or two or three. I was unraveling.

During the height of anarchy in my Bangkok life and in the political uprising, Central World and the channel three building were on fire while I used the distractions to get my fixes. The hotel in Manila reached out again, so impressed with our initial phone interview, to open up dialogue regarding their corporate chef vacancy. The role had been empty for two years and something about my slick mouth, high or not, appealed to the HR director in Manila enough for her to recommend me for the vacancy.

My phone rang during a busy afternoon at WTA with a number from the Philippines. Having the wherewithal to recognize the number pattern, I answered. The well-spoken and overly polite gentleman on the end was the hotel owner, Raxton Cacentaro, the youngest of a large family of wealthy Chinese/Filipinos whose family owned a large amount of assets throughout the Philippines including Philippine Airlines, Waterfront Resorts & Casinos, and a large city of industrial plastic mills. His family generated their wealth from by inventing a type of widely used plastic. He spoke candidly about my time in Bangkok and asked questions with the intent of listening. He wasn't just waiting for his turn to talk. One of the most obnoxious quips I'm known for saying is "listening does not mean waiting to speak." It was clear Sir Raxton, as is the common formal address in the Philippines, along with Po, grew his wealth and reputation with his ability to listen. I listened as well. I listened to his retort about how impressed he was with my experience and maturity as well as my earnest intentions on relocating at the pinnacle of political tension in Bangkok. At the end of our interview, or candid discussion, he offered me the vacancy of corporate executive chef. I had just turned thirty-one, my soon-to-be child was at the point where family could be informed, and my addiction was as rampant as I could ever recall. I immediately accepted the role without having an inclination to discuss the decision with Annie. Sir Raxton explained to me that I would be stationed in Cebu, to begin a new chapter of life with added responsibility. I had the opportunity to seek a geographical reprieve and arrest my addiction before it was too late. Little did I know methamphetamines were a raging epidemic in the Philippines, as was illegal prostitution - my two cruxes.

Awaiting the contract offer, unaware of what life ahead in the Philippines would be like for even a second, I finally discussed my new opportunity with Annie. I laid out the plan; I would take the role alone, at first, while she prepared herself for travel and worked on documents for importing the dogs with her. She would join me there at her latest available date to fly. I would take the first three months to get a new home ready for the arrival of Annie and our unborn baby. I wasn't leaving them behind. I left no option for dialogue, as was the case in most of my discussions while mired in active addiction. I spoke *at* people and never *to* people. I was directing Annie...my addiction was directing Annie.

Annie and I talked about discussing the next steps with her mother. Yai's (yai is the Thai word for grandmother) mental preparation would be needed and her approval would be necessary for the move. She was an old school, traditional Thai woman, meaning her understanding of life outside of Thailand was less than adequate. Most Thais just call foreigners 'Farang' regardless of your place of naturalization. I understood her capacity and was willing to work with it. We didn't want to brief her monotonous, sheltered existence for the inevitable move, but it was absolutely necessary. The three of us sat down during an afternoon at WTA, and Annie and I explained our intentions. Yai was accepting on the condition, as long as we got married. Her eyes got wide in anticipatory celebration. I quickly diffused her expectations down to reality. We were not getting married out of love, but more out of necessity for so many reasons even above and beyond our child. I countered her offer with a legal marriage, less the ceremony. I wanted my child, and myself, to avoid paternity tests and name changes if anything ever happened to either of us. I wanted Annie to be able to sign papers on my behalf for the dogs. I wanted my new employer to not frown on my "girlfriend" joining me. It was much more appropriate for a family to move borders, but as was the case with Niki, as you recall, marriage would have squashed all presumption. I wanted protection. It was smart.

The idea of marriage never once appealed to me, especially marriage with Annie. The thought of my child not immediately having a US passport and my last name was too scary to entertain the thought of. We agreed 10/10/2010 would be the date. I would start my contract in Cebu on 10/01/2010 and return for the signing.

It was more important to be back in Thailand for the 10th of October as it was my brother, sister, and sister-in-law's arrival date to Bangkok for a vacation that had long since been planned. Things were coming together, but my use of meth was crushing my soul....still. The self-serving agendas and maneuvering of my lifestyle to match and comply with my drug-controlled agenda is so clear, in hindsight, yet completely undetectable while being under the control of substance, to myself mostly.

Early October had arrived. Having now done the formal introduction and one week walkthrough with my new employer in the Philippines, Waterfront Hotels, I was looking forward to getting back to Bangkok to see my brother and sister. It had been three years since I'd seen them. A big part of me, or 'the other guy' as I so cavalierly refer to him, hoped to avoid them cramping my drug use. My sister-I'm-law, if you've been reading, could catch Ebola for all I cared, so I hoped she made the least negative impact an uppity cunt like Dee could make. That was as much as I'd ever be able to hope for from that bitch.

I had been clean by default for a week, but I was withdrawing after landing in Bangkok and went straight to Soi 3. I got my fix minutes after landing. My disease told me life was good. Anyone viewing it subjectively would argue that stance, and I had no argument that could honestly oppose it, but 'the other guy' inside me wasn't about to let me off the hook. Not until everything was on fire from the inside out would my addiction seek shelter.

Annie and I were late to get my family at Suvharnabum Airport in Bangkok. They care about shit like that - I take things as they come and manipulate the parts I can coerce. My family had been walking through my bullshit on stilts at this point for some years, but the years prior to me heading to Singapore were clean years, three to be exact. This being said, you could imagine the shame and disappointment I felt when they asked if "everything was ok with me." These are accusatory words to any self-absorbed addict complying with the orders of his or her addicted self. The two characters in my repertoire were so easily recognizable I was fooling myself by believing anything but. As it so happens, punctuality is one clear indication things are off with me, and my family knew it. I was off. On was as foreign a word as much as clarity was a foreign feeling. I sidestepped their accusation, as I felt it was, and went on clouded with ignorance. "I am fine, just worn from all the travel and emotional exhaustion," I said. Annie and I had been exchanging plan ideas and itinerary for my family's trip out to see me and meet Annie. We were scheduled, in my understanding, to sign our marriage doctrine shortly thereafter. Annie was dressed up. She looked cute. She was starting to show and put on baby weight, but that was and always has been more beautiful than the tiny, tight ass frames I loved throwing around the sack so much. It was strangely comfortable to be comfortable with Annie being pregnant.

As we went on through Bangkok traffic at a snail's pace that Saturday evening, I questioned Annie if the office was still open as it was now after five o'clock. She assured me there would be no way we were missing our appointment. I grew skeptical. My brother and sister and the uppity cunt, Dee, were all in our car, and we were talking about our plans for the next day. They, being privy to news I hadn't been privy to, explained they were tired too and ready to just get home after we stopped and signed the marriage certificate. Being high at the time, my addiction grew relieved at the thought that I could put my brother and sister right to bed and abscond for a couple hours to sneak in my adventurous, drug and sex induced double life for the night. Getting that guy his fix was now non-negotiable.

October 10th, 2010 ended up being a cover for the real marriage certificate signing and a fake anniversary. Our appointment was set the following afternoon in Koh Samui, Ampur (or city hall in Thailand). We never made it to the Bangkok, Ampur that night.

Annie slowly pulled into a banquet hall laced with fancy, freshly waxed and decorated cars. Some had pink bows across the hood while others were colored with white marker. "Congrats, Matt & Annie" was written on several rear windshields. Flower petals were artfully scattered about the entrance leading into the hall. I was duped. It was clear I was being taken to my OWN SURPRISE WEDDING! I was appalled and angered. I made it clear there was not to be any ceremony, but Yai, being a very old school Thai woman, wouldn't hear my instruction. She didn't care what I wanted and neither had Annie. This should have served as all the warning I would need to reconsider our arrangement, but being high and focused on getting through the next couple hours without my addicted self exposing himself propelled me into fight mode. My family, following with piqued curiosity and naivety towards the situation, as I rarely discussed the status of my love life or nuances that surrounded it, offered congrats and appeared to not only know where we had been headed, but in total support of this nightmare. I was in the fucking twilight zone.

As we swung open the double doors to a full banquet hall of clapping Asians, I felt as anyone would at their own fucking surprise wedding - overwhelmed and riddled with bafflement. I had never met anyone in Annie's family other than Yai. I mean, we broke up a week before baby oopsie, my Evelyn, was known to have been conceived. The mass of well-dressed strangers stretched to the very back of the hall, Annie, myself, and my family were shown to the head table, and I was immediately handed a microphone. Hell on Earth had taken on the most innocent cover. I detested public speaking and even more so when forced to do it in a language other than my first. There was no way I was getting out of this. My addiction screamed at me from inside the dark hole he was hibernating in while real me was left jilted, trying to get us through this. I made my speech cordial and brief, and passed the microphone to Annie covering the mouthpiece to shoot a look of death into her eye and whisper how fucking thrilled I was that they forbade and disregarded our agreement as to no ceremony. My addiction, hibernating for a couple hours but still on high alert, started to tally the benefits of Annie's boundary crossing and noticed all the envelopes Annie was receiving. My addiction told me they were mine, and even more so entitled to the contents of the envelopes for having endured this living nightmare. As the overly contrived and awkward ceremonies drew to a close, I made sure to keep all the envelopes in my possession. I explained, or my addiction explained, to Annie I needed some space and would appreciate her taking my family back to our flat and let them decompress and unwind. She agreed. The next few hours would be spent forcefully expelling the surprise wedding with copious amounts of methamphetamines and orgy filled sex fantasies. I used every dime from those envelopes. They were my prize for enduring the wedding night. It was also clear to me then that sustaining a marriage to Annie would have required an infinite number of money envelopes. The wedding night envelopes were how I would pay back the loan taken out on my pride that night. This was how my addiction took it out on me for putting him through such bullshit, as well.

Returning home early the next morning would set the tone for the rest of our illegitimate marriage. It would also provide Dee, also known as Cuntzilla, and Annie enough common ground to kindle a two-woman support group aimed at arresting my happiness at any juncture of life without cause, clean or not. That night was their cause. My careless, addicted self wrote some checks with his deplorable actions and unapologetic mouth and left sober me to cash them…perpetual, daily interest would be accrued and taxed until the day I die. This is pretty common in most addict's timelines. One of the two girls would, henceforth, manufacture the bullshit for the other's immediate purchase. If you're not minding your business in the US, you're clearly not doing it right…or so Dee thought.

The next morning we would take a single engine charter flight in a torrential downpour, which was common through October and November in Thailand. Our "honeymoon," as it turned out to be, was starting in Koh Samui, my first Thai stomping ground, before we jetted to Phi Phi for a night and ended on the more laid back beaches of Koh Lanta, a west coast island. Annie and I actually had a nice time, and my brother and sister did as well. The excursions away from Bangkok and my Soi 3 had arrested my use for a few days. Withdrawing once again and running low on money, Annie and I decided to cut it short and head back to Bangkok. We would say goodbye to my family and spend the next forty-eight hours going over the process to obtain the dogs' import permits as well as Annie's spousal visa to join me in a couple months in Cebu. I wasn't sure I had avoided being high around my family long enough to keep my family from briefing my parents on my current obliterated status, but that would be a bridge to cross when the time came.

The perception towards addicts in the minutia of the day-to-day simplicities, to the normal people, is actually pretty comical once I've had enough recovery time to look back and laugh at myself. My mind convinces me I've avoided an intervention while my head rejoices at the thought of having sidestepped an interruption to my use, while those that pray nightly for me and exhaust every nerve of patience to keep their composure long enough to not let me know they're onto me is a fragile dance. I never resented the people in my life that didn't know how to handle me at my worst, but I do resent those that still treat me with the same skepticism today. There is no correlation or common ground between the two people inside me. They detest each other, actually. My mother, years after my gallivanting ceased, told me of the countless nights she cried herself to sleep and about how she wore a line in her tongue from having had to bite it so frequently during our short Skype calls throughout the few years I had been abroad. Painful, I get it now.

5 | PHILIPPINES - 2011

As the plane touched down in Cebu, Philippines, I took everything in. Tagalog, the national language, was difficult to learn, but Filipinos knew much more English than Thais did. Most Filipinos spoke Tagalog, Visayan (central Philippines Tagalog dialect), Spanish, and English. I appreciated not having to be the dipshit foreigner in social circles off the jump. As the driver rambled on about how excited the group was to have a corporate executive chef back in the fold, I couldn't help but notice the overcrowded, seedy alleys and squatters in most neighborhoods...actually, in all the neighborhoods I drove through. The Philippines was overrun with poverty. Every city I went to lacked big city efficiency and structure. There were no city planners, no subways, no fancy cars, or even nice restaurants. The hotel I would be working out of, however, was grandiose in every sense of the word. It was the staple venue for anything worth noting that ever happened in Cebu, the central capital of the Visayas, which was also the central region of the 7,701 islands that made up the Philippines.

The hotel had thirty-foot ceilings and extravagant carpentry, and it looked more like a cathedral. There were five restaurants within the hotel, all of which had foreign executive chefs. The ballroom was as exquisite as the casino. Everything was majestic and extra. The iced lattes were served in fancy crystal and the daily buffet served lobster, house-made French pastries, and fresh noodles being hand-pulled center stage. The carpets were hypnotizing, and I could have run into a wall trying to follow the patterns in an OCD-like seizure. The corridors were deep and scattered with fine art and vivid, wavelike patterns laced with gold trim. I felt fancy. I was anything but.

As I walked up to the front desk of my new home, Waterfront Hotel & Casino, Lahug, to introduce myself with my meth-mouth preventing an authentic smile, I was told no introduction would be necessary. I still felt fancy and important. I was excited for my new role. I went right to my room and popped in my new SIM card to the BlackBerry phone that was part of my welcome package. I was excited to tell Annie about my latest adventure. I was still just disappointed that the person was Annie on the receiving end of my attention, as I had grown a huge distaste for even the site of her face, as it interfered with 'the other guy's' agenda....meth. Niki was a distant memory, but Annie wasn't even a suitable stopgap in my codependency.

I did feel a sense of freedom about having time to myself after such a long road over a couple years through Singapore and Thailand. It had been a progressively hastening downward spiral since I picked up a drink in Singapore back in 2008. That night in Geylang led me to a full-blown meth addiction two countries later and over two years later. It was about to turn 2011 and once again another resolution of getting well enough and fast enough to be a passable father and validate myself once again as a chef. I coveted time, without apology, to help quell the noise in my head. My career, as much as I jokingly self-deprecate, has been less than adequate, in all honesty, but that's by my own estimation and certainly not without some success. At this point in my career, I'd been graced with awards such as Restaurant of the Year from the Boston Globe in 2008 as Executive Chef of Keon's 105 Bistro, just before I left Boston for Singapore. In our first year, Beach Republic was mentioned as the thirty-first top destination in the world according to the New York Times yearly top forty destinations, globally. I spent my younger days cooking various stations in the kitchens of Todd English, Barbara Lynch, and several other notable chefs to learn and sponge up the education. I would moonlight in different restaurants around Boston just to learn other techniques and cuisines. A kitchen was and still is the only place in the world I'm one hundred percent guaranteed to find immediate comfort in. It's a visceral sanctuary. I never used drugs once in a kitchen. There was a deep level of self-motivation and just regular old enjoyment out of cooking. I moved fast into executive chef roles. I wasn't old enough to drink before I was an executive chef in Faneuil Hall, Boston.

My career was always something my most rigid critics would say I took for granted, and in retrospect, I admittedly had. I was, since as young as I could remember, untapped potential. The fulfillment and execution of my own visions were perpetually clouded by drugs. I managed to thrive without ever feeling as though I exhausted the resources and capabilities within my capacity because I folded like a cheap suit time and time again into the irrelevance imposed by drugs. Agonizing as opportunity lost to substance can be, I never regret what I could have done, and I have, by now, taught myself to appreciate the present, the now. These forms of gratitude are absent in the eye of active addiction. The intangible things I have in terms of integrity and virtue are self-taught through the practice of staying small and humble, words rarely, if ever, associated with my own assessment of myself or that of others. Yeoman's work for an addict is putting ourselves into situations we would otherwise avoid or fail in and finding the way. My new position was one I believe I normally, as my soul purports, thrive in through humility and fortitude and ultimately progressive success attributed to raw sweat ethic. The ability to be wrong and happy is unteachable to addicts, yet intuitively accepted in my sobriety.

Sports came naturally to me; I was an all-conference hockey player in high school in the greater Boston talent pool and an elite pitcher with several colleges looking to recruit my arm. I opted for fun, and that fun came in the lifestyle of high-end, fast-paced restaurants and the shenanigans and loose lifestyle they provided. I chose culinary school after a brief stint in state college. As I said earlier, a Ph.D. was not in the cards after a .37 GPA. My thirst for school and wealth and conformity was nil. Anyone aspiring to be a chef has to remove a lot of the normal life obligations and arbitrary contrivances that the normal people get to check the box on. It was perfectly fine to me. I was addicted to the feeling I got from the work I did. I was untouchable in any kitchen, as I told myself. The adrenaline rush after a night on the line operating in perfect harmony while creating dishes that made me proud to be a chef was indescribable and unattainable through any substance, or any other path. I saw only one path. I could recall just about any notable meal I'd ever had. My food and style were always approachable - my demeanor, not so much.

My first night in the hotel was comfortable - my first day on the job, not so much. As my introduction to the group and other chefs culminated, I could feel there was an obvious disdain with Sir Raxton having invited me into a role unoccupied for so long and desired by those fighting an uphill battle through their efforts over time in the hotel. I strolled off a plane from Thailand and sat at the culinary head. The executive chefs turned a blind eye to my existence or title and feigned support. They sabotaged every attempt I made at immersing myself amicably into the lives of those I worked with closely. The other chefs joined forces and offered a giant, immature bowl of cold shoulder soup. I have been told I carry a chip on my own shoulder at all times, but that is the version of me I work to lighten and improve upon. There is always resolve in my actions and intentions, although intense, feisty, and contentious are synonymous adjectives I have been said to carry as part of my character. I can't deny that, but I am aware of my effect on any situation. I gave up a long time ago defending this and accept it as part of my real character. It's the discernment in knowing where and when to apply the aforementioned traits into my daily life that separates the two people in me.

My objective, regardless of whether the 'junior varsity' chef's club accepted me or not, was not tied to the day-to-day operations of any of the hotels I oversaw. I was there to standardize the recipes of the hotel from the northernmost property in Manila to the southernmost resort-style hotel in Davao. I was assigned two lackeys that would grind it out with me for the length of my contract, as I deemed necessary. I was assigned to tasks that needed no cooperation with any other chef, and it would take me the year. I would be traveling at my own leisure, eating whatever I wanted for free, and getting chauffeured every step of the way. I was autonomous in my role, as Sir Raxton so informed the group, meaning the other chef's acceptance of me was irrelevant. They, much like subordinate officers in military rank, were obligated to follow my lead. Being a gracious winner was also not my natural inclination, so in reading my own words I start to retain it slowly.

I once had a boss sit me down as we recruited staff for a high profile restaurant opening in Boston. He had asked, "Matt, if ten people tell you that you're an asshole, you're an asshole!" I found this particularly ironic because the source was equally as deplorable and polarizing. He was right, but that's the pot calling the kettle black.

My geographical cure didn't manifest the way I'd hoped it would. Then again, if I was looking for a manifestation and not resolved to fighting tooth and nail with minute-by-minute intensity, I wasn't ready to attack it. I was passive in my approach. I relied on the expectation of not finding my drug of choice. I was foolish and unprepared. The impending arrival of Annie compounded with the stress that surrounds the birth of one's first child. The child was slated to arrive in early March, and I subconsciously turned my intention into self-loathing and discontentment. I would convince myself as I had without fail, or should I say without success, ad nauseam, that my efforts were there, and before long I would be selling and buying my own self-peddled bullshit again. I deserved to get high, didn't I? Maybe, but no one deserves the self-inflicted torture that follows, and I'm not one of the normal people that can apply the social use tactic. Pain, as humans, is inevitable; the suffering, however, is optional. Maybe it was the autonomous work schedule, or the fact that there is no such thing as a geographical cure, or maybe I truly would never be ok allowing myself to be happy and successful. I speculate, because it perplexes me. It consumes me and doesn't let go.

Leaving a poker hall in Lahug in late December of 2010, I met a group of guys who appeared to be of questionable character. Before the hour turned, I was in an hourly motel with a bag of meth and the finest selection of eighteen-year-old prostitutes the dodgy halls of Gate Three had to offer. Gate Three was a compound, like so many others scattered around the islands of the Philippines, that housed poor girls who worked in sex trade in hopes of sending a few pesos back to Mom and sometimes Dad, who were almost always the caretakers of said sex worker's children. Girls in the Philippines would have children as young as thirteen years old. They, too, at fourteen to seventeen years old, would commonly attempt to work in sex trade when they found a John willing to look the other way, or even worse, a pedophile by nature. The night I went back out with a thirst for meth and a hunger to quell the sexual deviant in me, just before Annie was set to join me, would take me down a long and dark hole that I still find myself digging out of ten years later. Every opportunity at making a positive impact was squandered. I always, as an addict should steadfastly maintain, welcomed a never-too-late attitude at exoneration. Unfortunately, I, like the rest, was at the literal mercy of the people I rode over during my addiction, and even at a larger level of earning pardon from those I backed up over and rode over twice.

Annie was booked to fly into Manila a few days before Christmas in 2010. My addictive behavior helped convince the true version of myself to push her flight back as many times as I could until the doctors in Bangkok gave Annie a hard deadline. I saw my fun ending, but 'the other guy' in me wasn't letting go. Annie had been working on getting the documents for Brownie and the two beagles, Herbie and Maya, ready so they could travel with her. Everything was ready, cages were bought, and we had just found out we would be having a baby girl. This motivated me, but my addiction didn't give a fuck. I attributed my still being alive to this point to my late grandmother and angel on earth, Evelyn. She was a crass old bag with a two-pack of Benson & Hedges and one-dollar scratch ticket habit. She was the reason I could pedal my ass on my BMX bike up to the store at nine years old and buy a pack of butts with a handwritten note. I loved her like no one else did - she was "my people." Of the three of us kids, I was the only one who ever spoke to her. I would help her clean up after her bowels gave out on her so I could keep my mother from sending her to assisted living. We played Gin Rummy and Crazy Eights and watched Unsolved Mysteries and Grand Ole Opry. We would argue and fight, but I was her favorite. I would argue and fight with anyone, and she would too. I never thought much about names for my child because culturally Annie and I, I presumed, would have different expectations. The moment Annie shared the news with me the only thing I could even muster from my mouth was "Evelyn." Annie agreed, though the Thai tongue would fall short in annunciating it. She most likely agreed because she heard the conviction in my tone and heard my voice crack. This was important to me.

We brainstormed Evelyn's middle name and thought it would be appropriate if it were a Thai word. Mali, the Thai word for Jasmine, couldn't have been a better fit. Evelyn Mail Garon was going to be my daughter's name. We both loved it.

As stressful as a journey can be when you're carrying a six-and-a-half-month pregnancy with you, imagine doing it with three dogs, immigration checkpoints, an overnight layover, and no help in sight. I was happy about the pups, and some part of my true self was relieved to have Annie with me, but my addiction was taking a stand, a hard stand. Credit Annie for having the perseverance to get to me. I was no help. I was living a life fully dependent on my next high and using a revolving door of young girls, and as many of their cute friends that wanted to join, for lust-filled sexcapades and escapes into a drug-induced fantasy lasting for days or weeks at a time. Annie was directed to stay home and incubate the nest. Even though our months leading up to rejoining each other were filed with fake promises and empty "I love you's," the face-to-face version was having trouble feigning affection. Annie, looking back, must have been horrified at the underweight, cynical, easily irritated, and always eager to fly off the handle version of the guy she knew in Bangkok once upon a time.

It's one thing to cleverly articulate my thoughts and intentions onto a page, but it was seemingly impossible to materialize those intentions into right actions throughout my day with any semblance of balance of consistency. I truly wanted a friendship and the ability to openly communicate that with Annie, avoiding contentious vibes, as co-parents. I think we would both desperately cling to our implied rights as parents with a fierceness that a child warrants. Being born out of love is unfathomable to me but being born out of the reciprocity in love between two adults was easy to grasp at that point. I didn't love Annie, and it was becoming harder and harder to hide it.

I did show Annie to our new home after she touched down in Cebu. It was an awkward and bittersweet moment. Things in me had changed and things certainly did in her. In my mind, providing what I was responsible for - a home, food, and attention - were harder and harder to maintain. I was fortunate my employer took care of most of my living circumstances.

I had found the home Evelyn would be born into shortly before Annie arrived. Up until this point I was living out of my hotels and too busy to be bothered with that stuff. It was a four-story, Spanish-style home overlooking the rolling hills in northern Cebu - a white villa with orange roof shingles, four bedrooms, and a maid's quarters. The house was beautiful. We were, however, in a secured compound with Calderon Cock Fighting Pit at the entrance to the compound. This would help me understand later why the price was vastly lower in contrast to others comparable in size and location. We would hear the screams of the bettors and roosters as the cocks duked it out every Sunday for supreme alpha. The fireworks were incessant, and karaoke was a popular household activity. It was hardly tranquil, but it was home. I spent very little time there, and even less after Annie arrived. My addiction lied to me. It told me I was better off staying in my hotels to get my work done, and then it would invite me out for week-long adventures that left me broke and scorned back home. Annie scolded me for not having rent money, shopping money, and even money just to eat at times. It was clear Annie wasn't happy from the start, but my addiction egged me on, justified my waning efforts, and convinced me we were doing just fine. We weren't. I wasn't.

It had been over two months since I saw her, and by now she was over six months pregnant. She was overly fatigued from being my life administrator as it pertained to the dogs in order to keep them with us through the move. I couldn't accept or envision being alone in any home with Annie and not having the distraction of another beating heart. The dogs were my diversion. Annie had to have both the beagles vaccinations forged for international export. She did it for me.

My time, as my addicted self-justified, was devoted to Waterfront and the objective I proposed to the company was instantly accepted for rollout. I was working on a software-based recipe guide system with a web-based server in our central Visayas location. My work was remote, but my attention and allotted time to

Annie and Evelyn in the third trimester would be nonexistent. I lied to myself to continue the destructive path I was on. I was unaccounted for by those that paid my salary and left to my own self-addicted will. My time, by now, was reserved for whatever my drug allowed it to be reserved for. My decisions were no longer mine.

As time drew nearer to Evelyn's expected arrival, March 8, 2011, Annie was dealt a raw deal. I would say "we" were dealt one, but I celebrated the nights my job would keep me away from our home. My southernmost property, Waterfront Davao, was struggling to keep balance. The executive chef would need to be released from his duties, and I would have to cover his role while working remotely on my project until a new chef was recruited and trained. This, leaving only one month until the due date, as it was now early February, would pose a challenge to getting back to Cebu for Evelyn's birth. Waterfront knew my situation, and we ultimately discussed things and thought it best to have Annie induced into labor and schedule a specific set of days where I could be back in Cebu to see through Evelyn's birth. Annie did her due diligence as she always had and found a doctor corrupt enough to take our request and honor it. Evelyn was going to be scheduled for induced labor on March 3, 2011. I loved the date, as I selected it, because 3/3/2011 seemed impossible to forget. Pretty sad, I get it. I left the correspondence between Annie and the doctor to them. I was extremely busy in my own diluted mind, but I probably should have opened an email attachment or two.

In addition to now being less than thirty days from Evelyn's arrival, I was coordinating the arrival of my mother and Annie's mom, Yai, to be with us for that week. They would be there, as they thought, to meet their grandchild. My logic was for them to be present when my addiction called me away. I was ashamed. It was evidently clear that Evelyn was not being born into a clean or loving home. We have involuntary self-perceptions and projections in our minds, I was no different, but this was not one of the projections I had ever or was ever prepared for. The progressively widening quagmire I was frantically trying to crawl out of was seemingly impossible. I woke up every day begging God, a stroke of chance, or some diving intervention, to help me arrest my addiction for long enough to make a positive, well-aimed decision that I could piggy back off of. The prayer wasn't answered. Not in Evelyn's time, at least. It's always answered - it's just not typically the response an addict is prepared or equipped for.

Valentine's Day of that year, less than three weeks from Evelyn's scheduled flush, would be one that saw me prioritize the call girl of the week over my own wife. The daily grind of pipes, foil, crystal meth, and young girls spun me into a fantastical vortex of self-destructive shenanigans. I never had remorse after using drugs or people because their attention was what my addiction sought. My addiction fueled my entitlements to use. 'the other guy' was running things, and I was his bitch. I justified my actions predicated on my misguided intentions and, furthermore, my presumption into the lives of those I've used…the toxic leading the toxic.

The actions of any individual are clear-cut - right and wrong or fucking irrelevant. The reasons why they chose the action they chose have many steps to purity. When we first get clean the reasons to not act addictively or in poor character are simply not wanting to re-enter a self-induced struggle against the demon we just quieted. As we heal we go through several stages that hopefully lead us to the most important reason. It's because we didn't think to even act that way. My addiction subjugated my authentic self. I would be buying iPhones and jewelry for random hoes while spending every last peso long before the next check was coming. I rarely paid a bill. Meanwhile, my alleged wife sat back at home, eight months pregnant, scared, and in a foreign country. I had no empathy. What I had was a team of escort girls, all intent on the same thing, providing me service and getting high, in every city I had to spend time in, and wherever my work or avoidance of Annie took me. I thought this was the pinnacle of biological existence. I was sick and getting sicker. My drug didn't need me getting motivated to be a decent human. I was, at one point, a decent human.

I am, through constant practice and reflection, well-assessed in my own eyes. That's not to say I have no flaws or even few flaws. It's just my own ability to know who I am and to have an understanding how others perceive me, albeit not in the moment of passionate debate or dialogue, but in general, I understand my intense nature. I understand when my feelings are self-seeking and misaimed. It's the only way an addict can manipulate the heady people. The mindfulness to listen with my ears and not my mouth and knowing myself, considering every potentially grave flaw moment to moment, is what separates statuses of addicts and allows me to walk on entitled waters throughout my trashy addicted hell. I've developed an innate ability to never be given a real "no," and then lived with it. That's what's made my roller coaster of paternal terror so fucking surreal.

Evelyn Mali Garon was born on March 4, 2011, twenty-six hours after Annie was induced into labor, and six hours later than I would have liked. My mother and Yai had flown in with some weird bloke named Uncle Marvin. Marvin would say "hi" the first day, upon landing, and next time we would see him was at the airport on the way out. Strange man, but it looked like he had some fun in the Phils.

Back to Evelyn - no matter the most impactful and overly appropriate word you could find in any dictionary in any language, there isn't a word, expression, meme, quip, query, action, demonstration, or known noun or adjective otherwise that can accurately depict the feeling a parent has in seeing their baby for the first time. March 4, 2011 at 6:40AM in Cebu Drs. Hospital, Cebu, Philippines, I experienced what the hype was all about. It crippled me and still does. The best drug on earth is pure happiness. As much as others provide that happiness, I will never feel deserving of it. You could explain it a million times and have me do a million test runs for accepting sustained, pure happiness, and it will hit me the same way on the first day as the last. Give me a kitchen, however, and I will at least forget my pain – it is self-induced, but it is pain, nonetheless. The most fearful moment in any human's life is the moment that surreal feeling dissipates, and we're left with our impending reality. Evelyn is my reality, and as I said, my purpose. That will go unchanged until I'm but a ball of Massachusetts dirt.

Shifty moves, or my "hustle" as it's widely called, was how my addiction fed itself. Quite often that hustle would lead me to situations that made sober me blush. Most people talk about shit they want to do, have done, or know someone that has done, but few actually talk in proportion to what they have to offer versus gain. Most over promise and under deliver. In my addiction I am all talk and, in contrast to sober me, finds myself coming to many people's underestimated surprise - back to self-assessment being essential. It's extremely difficult to learn when you're not trying to. The empty words of an active addict aren't just painful to the ones they affect. They are harmful to us, too.

Self-loathing is gross - I judge it hard. I judge myself equally, I think. I am constantly pulling my mind back from the natural path to "poor fucking me."

Evelyn's birth was quick. I wasn't ready. Reality came back around hours after she was born and I was getting ready to sweep us all out the back door of the hospital and home after having to explain to my mother that I had barely enough money to cover the bill. I didn't have any money, but I was hoping to avoid anyone knowing that. See, in the Philippines, if you don't pay, you don't leave. As we got to the ground floor Annie, Evelyn, my mother, Yai, and I were met by the doctor's nurse. She asked me to come to the payment window and settle my bill. I had no money, and my mother knew it. She actually overheard me pleading with the nurse and offered to pay, but I was not about to borrow more money. I was embarrassed and defensive, mostly from the emotional instability the drugs caused. I got to the cashier's window and explained I could not pay the doctor's fee. It was unknown to me what it was, because I never checked my email, but I knew it would be presented. I hoped otherwise, but here I was staring the embarrassment and ridicule of not being able to pay the doctor in a third world country right in the face. All because I didn't hit click and open the email? No, because I'm an addict. The circumstances and headwinds are all because I'm an addict.

I was sick to my stomach. Evelyn was less than twelve hours old, and I put her in a situation. Within minutes of refusing to pay, armed soldiers and other hospital personnel guarded the exits. The cashier implored me to find a money transfer or cash otherwise and the soldiers, who the cashiers spoke to in Tagalog, were told to stand their position and prevent us from leaving. I did what I knew and that was to maintain my stance, adamantly and completely wrong. Wrong, and if I was going to be wrong, I was going to be obnoxiously wrong. I went full Karen on the hospital staff, telling them who my employer was and threatening to call the US Embassy, as if they would ever do anything, anyway. My family, Annie and her mother, as well as my mother were hanging their heads shamefully. Eventually my call to the US Consulate in Cebu struck the cashier and hospital personnel and armed guards to stand down and let us be on our way. We all left and never spoke of that again.

They say in self-help circles that you hit your bottom when you stop digging. I was digging deep and still not done. Every time I recollect this moment it levels me. Humility is essential for an addict. Evelyn knows today about this debacle at the hospital. It's like being brought back from the dead when you see the uncontested, gargantuan love on your child's face searing the feeling back into your soul. She's forgiven me, as I have myself.

After the first few nights of Evelyn's life in the Philippines, our parents were headed home - my mother to Boston and Yai to Bangkok. My last couple days with my mother were somber. There were few words that anyone could say to trump or dampen the happiness Evelyn's birth brought me, anyway. My condition proved what my mother feared without us needing to discuss it. My mother never would discuss the specifics of anything, but she would just make her intuitive 'understanding' of my situation known with a sympathetic, "We're all here for you if you need us." They got me. My mom got me. My parents are the reason I'm alive, biologically and through direct and indirect acts of love. Their influence on my good character is obvious, while they work harder than any parent could be asked to work and do it more willingly and selflessly than any parent should be expected to be. My entire life tested their ability to feel good about their efforts. It's not them…it's me.

I was heading back to Davao in a couple days to resume holding up a sinking ship, but it was my ship, and my addiction still needed to be fed. Leaving Evelyn the first week was hard. If only I knew. Annie and I were distant as we had been since breaking up some lifetimes ago. I could tell she resented me for bringing her here by now. Annie was still recovering from the C-section and the physical and emotional struggles leading up to Evelyn being born. It wouldn't be long before my contract ended, but Annie maintained we all would be coming to the US, as we planned back in Bangkok. I could see my destruction hardening her and challenging her decision at every opportunity. The dogs were starting to get on Annie's nerves, and I was stuck hundreds of miles away. I tried to stay clean. I shattered again. I was starting to feel like I would never be clean. As my Davao project got new life and opened some spending, I found a chef worth recruiting. I could finally head back to Annie and Evelyn and apply my time mostly in transit while trying to finish my web-based recipe guide system. I had diversion and purpose. There was huge money invested into this project.

As my contract drew near expiration in June of 2011 and my work was stagnant, our HR director gave me a call regarding the renewal of my next contract, or so she said. We would agree to discuss an extension in a couple weeks - once I got my data encoded to the server for the hotel's entire recipe guide system. I had yet to start encoding, and it would take weeks. Years at the pace I prioritized it. The only thing I took from this was their willingness to renew my contract. I felt my demon already contemplating our next self-inflicted debacle.

A few days later, I had just gotten back to Davao after seeing our owner for a brief meeting in the northern offices. It was a Friday morning around ten in the morning. I had just checked in to Waterfront Davao after landing from Manila. The hotel I stayed in was our boutique unit in Manila, and I had been using meth as I did in most rooms I stayed in. Random girls were constantly in and out and on the hallway cameras as regularly as a nurse doing rounds on her hospital patients. I could be seen in any hotel I was staying having arguments, eating unrealistically large meals, and leaving used condoms and crumpled up foil wherever I was. I had taken every opportunity to not pass by or to visit anyone of importance or even book my travel with any other corporate officer, as that usually cut into my play time. I required privacy by this point. I was using meth around the clock with a three-month-old Evelyn back home with

Annie, whom had given up on me weeks into Evelyn's life when I started to sell off everything in our house for obvious drug money. I sold everything except Evelyn's stuff.

As I landed in Davao after the meeting the previous night in the northern hotel, I had a voicemail from our corporate HR director asking me to call back immediately. When she answered she sounded a bit bashful and apologetic. I listened with intent as she started to ask me if I had ever heard of or used a drug they refer to as Shabu, or crystallized methamphetamine, as I knew it. I refused adamantly any knowledge or understanding of its existence in as "aww shucks" of a tone as I could muster. She asked if I could head to our local HR office at the hotel in Davao to accompany our manager to the clinic to do a drug screen. The two housekeeping attendants that were cleaning my room up north had found foil and crystal shards on my nightstand. I was getting sloppy, and it was all about to come back full circle. That moment I hung up, I was suffocating with fear and anxiety. I wasn't ready to lose my job or child.

Jonu Tan, my Davao sous chef, was a friend. I knew he didn't use drugs. I had a plan. I was the corporate officer running five hotel's F&B programs. I wasn't about to let this tiny lapse in focus cost me everything. I made a living off of being loved by my staffs and slippery to catch. I never anticipated having to ask one of them for a friendly bottle of their piss, but I did. Jonu just looked at me after I asked him for a bottle full of piss and said, "But I drink like a fish, Chef, Is that ok?." One thing about Davao at the time; it was governed by a family of hardened killers. Mayor, now President Duterte, was executing anyone caught with drugs in Davao, on site! This did little to dissuade me.

"Yes, Jonu, that is perfectly fine," I said.

Fucked up thing about that is, there are so many other moments that rival that one in deplorability. Several years later my business partner would reference my actions as "morally flexible." I wasn't crazy about euphemisms, but this one I'll keep. I really enjoyed hanging out with the Davao staff. Several members of that staff have gone on to have extensive travel and fast-tracked success. It never worked against me that I would always welcome a department basketball game and spend time cooking with them whenever I was around. I was always approachable and verbally inappropriate. This is chef charm. I would go to their karaoke nights and embarrass myself without a worry. They were just happy I was there. I recall even one chef and I getting a VIP room at a shower parlor together after a large event at the hotel and passing around and sharing six or so young ladies.

Jonu, without hesitation, went and relieved himself and handed me the small bottle he managed to replace the large bulky thermos I had given him first with. If it wasn't Jonu, anyone else that wasn't using would have sufficed and been willing. The problem for me was finding someone I suspected was clean. Just about everyone working a respectable job in Davao was clean, thanks to the then Mayor. Jonu and I would agree to take that to the grave later that day. Sorry, Jonu!

Somewhere in my mind, none of what's happened to me through my last few years seems unnatural in any way. Reality check - I was driving to the lab, policed by my HR director, with a bottle full of some other dude's piss in my sock and a two-month-old baby at home. It was not the portrait of normal or stability. Father of the Year would have to wait most likely too.

I went into the lab with a confident swagger and poured the piss from one cup to the next, handed it to the tech, and went on my merry way. The negative lab screen I pulled off was my free ticket until the end of my contract, or so I thought. I even pre-meditated my rebuttal assault on HR in my heightened, white privileged rage for putting me through such nonsense when the negative results came back. My piss was a dirty pool of disgust, but I wanted to buy my own bullshit. I believed every lie my addiction told me. Once HR called with my results, which happened hours later, I felt good and refrained from a counter strike to remain as invisible as possible. Addiction beat me into submission. It isolated me. It took me away from what I needed to thrive and get well.

My falling out in the Philippines would be right around the corner. Annie and I were down to speaking only when I appeared back at home, which was weekly for a couple hours. Some weeks I would be broke earlier and home with a withdrawing body.

I would still spend all my time at home taking Evelyn on walks, talking to her, putting my hat on her and seeing her get pissed and rip it off. I had no other desire other than to be with her. Annie would just give me a passing nod and a shameful glance as I lifted Evelyn out of her bassinet and walked out the door. I, carrying Evelyn, would walk up and back down the windy hill of the compound. She loved looking at the flowers, mint bushes, and anything that contained moving water. I told Evelyn my struggles and told her I expected her to do the same when she's old enough. I would bring her to the cashew tree to keep her shaded so I could tell her I was sorry for being the way I was - the dad I wanted to be versus the dad I was. I told her I expected more out of myself and that she deserves that. I told her I would be there for every boyfriend and every heartache. I told her I would never be that heartache. I told her I would be better, for her. She looked at me with intent when I talked, to the point I convinced myself she understood every word.

I didn't know much about being a responsible father, regardless of my drug-induced feelings and well-aimed intentions. I had been in a progressively deteriorative condition for three and a half years. The wife I never wanted now hated me, for good reason. I had little knowledge of how to parent, and my drug addiction was running my day from wake up to closing, if we closed at all that day. I was ready for a change.

In late-May, when an alarming amount of my "bottoms"

seem to take place, during that same year, I had a planned stay at that same boutique hotel I had accusations from. They were the first hotel to receive the touch screen monitors designated for each one of the twenty-six kitchens I oversaw. Do you want to know what a full-blown addict sees? I saw an opportunity to take the all-in-one computer and pawn it. It sounded like a good idea at the time. That's the sickness. I took the monitor into a taxi while tucked under my jacket, as if no one noticed me carrying anything. I told the HR manager at the hotel I was getting it fitted for waterproofing – this was clever and believable. I went out that night and got the usual case of punishment disguised in beautiful crystal shards and eager, young, pretty, addicted girls. I had been using just to feel normal again, and the drug was losing its effect. That night I knew the jig was up. If they weren't going to fire me because I stole the damn computer and lied about where it was going and then didn't return it, then I was going to just stop going to work and see how long before they knew I was gone.

I fled back to Waterfront Davao on a plane the next morning, avoiding oncoming calls and texts from the HR manager I blatantly lied to hours before. I knew it would be a difficult conversation. Once I landed in Davao, the driver was unusually quiet. He made no eye contact. I could smell an ambush. I redirected him back to the airport and scoured flights back to Cebu. I turned off my Blackberry and ended up walking through my door about eight hours later.

Night had fallen. Annie was at the door with an obvious panicked look. Evelyn was crying. Her crying made me irate - irate with myself. Annie came to the door and explained that my corporate HR counterpart and local HR manager had been to the house and were very worried about me. Annie had been crying. The noise in my head was desperate and all over the place. My decision settled on calling my parents, once again, and asking them to bail me out. I wanted to take a red eye to Manila, recover the computer, and return it to the hotel as if nothing ever left. My addiction was obviously still calling all the shots.

My parents, who knew what I was up to, reluctantly agreed to send enough for my travel, recovery, and return travel to Cebu. The condition was that I go back to the States right after. Annie had yet to apply for her visa, so she interjected what she really planned all along, and let me know she was going to Bangkok with Evelyn. I was desperate for everything, pulling me in every direction. Trying to think rationally was sporadically successful. I agreed to go back and start the process of coming clean and getting clean. My addicted self kicked and screamed. He told me I was sabotaging him, and that we would never be as happy as we were then. He's a fucking loser.

I left on a red eye that night after collecting my money transfer. Annie was going to be my parents' point of contact while I carried out my plan. Everyone knew what a pocketful of money does to an addict. I was scared to have the money myself. I made it to

Manila - then to the pawn shop at seven in the morning. I still had enough money to book a flight back to Annie and start my process to get us out of the Philippines. Then I heard that voice. I was now justifying my one decent action as grounds to get high. I knew it was sick. It was not an option, and I didn't want it...that's how I know it's a disease. I wanted to pull myself out of this other guy's hypnosis. It's like looking at your own life from the pit of your stomach with one of those endoscopy cameras and not being able to do anything. It's a helpless and hopeless existence. Ironically enough, a reverse endoscopy creates more nausea than the standard one. I figured that I could take the late flight back that day, drag out the time it actually took to return the computer, hit the poker room, make enough money to have one last crystallized hurrah, and get a couple of escorts to balance my great deed done that day. I never liked sitting down to play poker with the intention on winning money. It never worked out that way. I died anyway, because I convinced myself I needed to and deserved to. I was wrong quite often, looking back.

Within an hour I was broke. I fell off the map, disappearing into the steamy Manila streets on a blistering afternoon that quickly turned into evening. I walked and thought who I could swindle and what angle I could hustle. The jig really was up. By the time I built up the nerve to call my parents and Annie, they already knew. I was supposed to have touched base with them earlier. The shame in those phone calls is deafening. It opens up the "If you think that's fucked up, watch this!" gene.

I found leaving the Philippines a lot more difficult than arriving in the Philippines. In order to leave I would need to have my resignation letter approved by HR and Annie, because she would be taking Evelyn with her. She had to be approved for exiting the country with just a Thai passport for Evelyn. Her US passport was delayed by the doctor's refusal to sign Evelyn's birth certificate, thanks to our little snafu at the hospital on day one. Funny, I have actually found entirely new and untapped bottoms.

I was still stranded in Manila and had thrown my BlackBerry away by this point. I sent my resignation letter to HR and forgot to ever log back in to that email. My parents had bought me a ticket to Boston and Annie, with Evelyn, a ticket to Bangkok. I was in such poor condition that I refused going back to Cebu to even say goodbye to Evelyn and Annie. I never got to see my Brownie one last time. Herbie and Maya had a litter of perfect little pups. I sold them off to support my drug habit, so they gave up on me too, but Brownie never did. Evelyn, I knew I would see again. Annie told me she found a breeder in the Philippines that agreed to care for the dogs. It crushed me. I was polluted with shame. Annie and I talked briefly. She knew I was determined in my fight, but no doubt overmatched. We agreed I would check in at home and make a few bucks, clean up my act a bit, and rejoin my "family" that I was clinging to for the sake of not feeling completely alone. Realistically, Annie had been alone in the Philippines for six months. Evelyn was with her for three of those months. Shame was inevitable, but again, suffering is optional.

I landed back in Boston in July of 2011. Drugs had made me paranoid and abrasive on my best day. I look back and reminisce in horror the days and nights I saw my parents go through, and the ones I had heard about with disappointment and pain in my father's tone. I had never found meth in the US before, and I wasn't going to try then. The recovery started that time on the plane. I was feeling empty without Evelyn, feeling empty because of the way I handled myself in the past year and pretty much throughout most of my time in the Philippines, and Asia all together.

6 | THE CYCLICAL TORTURE – MARLBORO, MA, JUNE 2011

As I waited for my luggage I thought about the dogs; their new life was starting. I had to accept the fate I handed them and myself. Evelyn and Annie were the last to leave the Philippines. Their flight was leaving around the time I landed in Boston. Everything I did was selfish and inconsiderate. My mind was frantic just about every hour of the day trying to figure out how to get out of my own way. I tried Skyping and sending what I could for money the first couple of weeks, but Annie was still crushed from my deterioration in our young relationship. I tried to keep contact. Annie was still hoping I would turn the corner. No longer for her, but for Evelyn. Annie wasn't always a bad mother, but she was hardened. Too crushed to carry on small talk or to allow me a ray of hope to squeeze myself desperately back into their lives without first finding myself again.

I found a job quickly. It was for a new, high-end seafood restaurant that needed legitimacy and was willing to pay for it. I was obviously less than forthcoming with my new boss about my long-term intentions, but I had to do what I had to do. Once I had enough money to get to her I would. At this point in my career, being back in the US, with an international résumé and some youthfulness still aglow, most interviews were locks for a job. I decided I would join a privately owned former fish-and-chip shack turned high-end dining concept. The owner was Greek and stubborn. His wife was always more than friendly with me too. She liked to feel cute, and George, her husband and my boss, was oblivious. He ran his restaurant to the bareness one pretends not to notice while a restaurant is going down in a fiery mess. His wife, Elenia, would just come for her strokes and my attention.

I was coming in to absorb the verbal blows from indignant guests that just had their long-time fried fish joint turn into a foo-foo kind of place. That's how some ox-like, fat ass, bar hopping dickhead told me he found my food to be some years before. He pointed in disgust at a dish that was too artistic for his socially awkward ass to dive into and motioned it away, saying it was too 'foo-foo' for Haverhill, Massachusetts. That was the last move he made before I was pulling off his toupee and throwing his veal tenderloin in his fat, curly headed fuck face. It had been years since I saw him, but he and his spirit were alive in every guest we seemingly sat. I was also there to make the restaurant a success. Time was crucial, as it was in most of the positions I now looked to occupy. I had proven that idle time and lack of structure are too risky. I needed to keep something together, for Evelyn.

The immediate need was to bring new clientele into the restaurant and lighten the over-serious lingering air in the restaurant. I dove into my work. I had been commuting daily from my parents' house, which was a forty-five-minute drive to the restaurant, so before the first month was up, I was moving in with one of my cooks across the street from work. I was back to pretending my job was splitting atoms or curing cancer. And, although I had never found meth in the US up until this point, it didn't mean I was willing to live with my emotional anguish. I started smoking Percocet 80s every couple hours. I was drinking, investigating the prostitution scene in the US, and smoking weed every hour of the day. I was still flaking on my bills and rent. I still remembered every day what a shitty person and even worse father I had been. Clarity and sobriety looked good on me - great on me, to be honest. If only it lasted more than a week or two. The move out of my parents' house was propelling another round of self-destruction. My disease was a very poor decision maker.

As I cruised through new menu rollouts and hammered out prep, my passion for food was back. I was making some of the best dishes of my life. I was at the pier just about every morning. Some trips were hurried in order to get back with enough time to face the dinner rush, and some trips were educational to soak in what was coming in good, moving off season or low quality, and profitable. There's no benefit in having amazing dishes without being able to pay the bills. The restaurant grew up quickly. We were hosting the Phantom Gourmet and things had seemingly turned around.

Things in my living situation and personal life were stagnant. I was working up to down and I was hanging out after work nightly, with any free time I had, with a bartender that looked just like, if not even more handsome, than Tom Brady himself, and my roommate Shane. Shane was a troubled dude. Shane basically did whatever I told him - even pay all the rent. He was an insecure kid striving to be accepted. He was from the area and without a father. This I took note of more frequently. He was a product of an abusive home. I would hang out with 'Fake' Brady, Shane, and 'Fake' Brady's girlfriend, Kat. Kat and 'Fake' Tom Brady had a very unhealthy relationship. He was clean other than a raging bout of alcoholism and Kat drank with him, but she was recovering from heroin. These guys and Kat were fun, and they were helping me keep my mind off of Evelyn and being away from her. Kat either really enjoyed getting shit on by me or the fact that I was an aspiring junkie, as well, because our friendships all ended in one fell swoop with my penis in Kat's mouth while high on heroin and Andrew standing over us is disbelief and tears. I had enough implosive moments by now to know when I hit a low enough spot to move on. Staying up was just impossible. I used the incident to take my "out" at work after four months of being back in Massachusetts and, despite the outcome, a very productive job with the restaurant. I would use my final pay to get high, just after I paid for my ticket back to Bangkok. I was trying to do the impossible....out run myself.

The Duke of Doucheville

7 | BANGKOK – ROUND 2 - 2012

I was heading back to Bangkok on November 1, 2011. Evelyn was almost eight months old. We had been able to Skype, and Annie was starting to come around. She even told me they loved me at one point.

Evelyn was walking already. She just wasn't a baby that was going to be ok confined to her little space on the floor. We have shocking videos of her at six months and eighteen days old propping herself up with her arms to hold onto a sofa in order to start walking around Annie's quaint, two-bedroom apartment. Evelyn had my drive and fortitude. She was amazing. She still is just as amazing! Credit that same book, Outliers, that I referenced earlier. Christopher Langan, the then smartest man on the planet, for claiming his rights to genius status, citing his ability to walk at six months old. I was hoping that Evelyn's self-motivated progress was only a sign of things to come from her.

I was partly excited and wholly relieved that I had been free from meth for so long, but I had been medicated otherwise, and I could taste my next high in the back of my throat once I bought my plane ticket. It's as if my addiction lurks patiently in the rear until it sees an opportunity. My four plus months back with my parents and family wasn't nearly enough, but I wasn't well without Evelyn. I needed to be her dad. She needed me. Annie needed my help. I was airborne.

Upon landing back in Bangkok, I had very little money. I had reached out prior to getting back there with a former GM at WTA, who was now GM at an international fast casual company. They had four brand concepts - Coffee World, a knockoff Starbucks concept, was their focus as I was returning. I would manage to work out an arrangement that kept Annie working, as she wanted to do, and then myself earning as well through this new consultancy. I would have to accept one-third of my normal salary for Annie to be fully employed with the same salary for a separate employer. Annie was set to work at Asia Books Co., the Barnes and Noble of Thailand. She was thrilled at the new opportunity and was making great money for someone who was a Thai national. The average Thai salary was about fifteen thousand THB, or around four hundred and fifty dollars per month. Foreign salaries started around the equivalent to four thousand dollars. We would both make equivalent to one thousand dollars per month with the condition that my employment be a month-to-month consultancy. I accepted, knowing Annie would at least be in great position for years to come, in theory.

Granted, I needed to sacrifice my own salary for Annie to have hers, but it made everyone happy. Coffee World, as it turns out, was just looking to use my still dashingly handsome appearance to coerce a younger demographic and prove their legitimacy as far as foreign/Thai businesses are concerned. Having a foreign chef meant that you could afford a foreign chef. This attracted younger Thais. Malls and shopping plazas and restaurants were always full in Bangkok. The air conditioning is what dictates the attendance. Southeast Asia, as I alluded to, is eighty degrees Fahrenheit while it's nightfall. It gets between ninety and one hundred every day, and there is no cold. The closest I ever saw it get to chilly was during October and November when flood-like rains nourish the landscape.

We would all be staying in Annie's cramped apartment, choking on dust mites that had encased her furniture in black, web-like buildup. Evelyn had a cough. Yai was leery of me, and Annie was still not fully convinced I was ok. I was still not fully convinced I could be a father. The first few days there I had a chronic cough. I was still tasting meth in my mouth. Evelyn was walking. Holding her, hoisted in my arms with a baby arm draped around my shoulder while the other one cradled her exposed side and her cheek pressed so sweetly into my pec, was my place in the world. It was exactly the moment I knew where my place was. It was the unquestionable vulnerability we shared with each other. It was with Evelyn.

Evelyn and I would spend our days in the R&D lab at my

new consultancy. The girls from the office would always offer to watch her while I was meeting with cooks and food scientists to discuss specifics of dishes and go over product orders, often citing my inexperience as the reason. Really it was Evelyn's irresistibly cute face. Thais loved mixed race babies, and Evelyn was breathtaking from day one.

Evelyn would cry incessantly if she was away from me.. I was getting used to having her with me. I felt more "badass" doing that than anything I'd ever done in my life. We took the subway around Bangkok and stopped at random places to get to know the city more and more. I talked a lot…I still do, anyway. We ventured out of our habits and our comfort zones. During our time at home, Annie would pick up some dinner, and we would eat and watch Sesame Street with Evelyn while Yai did laundry. We were living out the start of family life, or at least a weak attempt at one. I was never decided one way or another with Annie when I thought about whether or not she would follow through with her US visa. I just wanted to get Evelyn to the States as fast as I could. That was where the problem lay. I would carry on oblivious to this, rather than adapt the plan to work best for all of us and preparing Evelyn for the most opportunistic path. The path Annie and I were reluctant to discuss was the path we knew opposed each other's vision - the entire path. Annie, by this point, feigned affection herself, and I could tell was just as unsure about me as she was in the Philippines. I never blamed her or anyone for keeping an eye on me, but she was sending her poor old mother around Bangkok trailing my every move. I would be several train transfers away from our home and run into Yai... coincidentally, of course..

This made me more scared than angry - scared I was losing Evelyn. I was scared I was being watched so intently with the expectation of failure. My mind would always revert to defensiveness. I trained it, or tried in my sobriety to train it to respond differently. I learned how to respond and not react through recovery. Training my mouth to stay shut was a totally separate matter. The difference in our mind's ability to discern what our natural reaction to something of someone is, acknowledge it, and move forward without our feelings interfering with what we knew was right, is responding. I recognized and acknowledged that anger, impatience, and jealousy are symptomatic of my disease. My response was me, authentically. My reaction was undoubtedly the opposite, or at least a long way off. My reaction was offended at life in general. Being able to feel at ease with my ability to respond appropriately to life as it unfolded was my gauge to myself. I was sober, but my addictive behaviors persisted. My addiction wasn't letting go. Even while I was making home life work and doing my best, as I could, free and clear from drugs, I was still an outcast. I felt as though Yai was getting more and more skeptical of me. Annie was working and late a bit, and I was doing goofy photo shoots for some failing company. I lived simply, yet this bothered Annie. I sacrificed my career so she could start one. I was offended. My addiction fought my ability to reason and see things clearly. I stayed clean, but I was not mentally prepared for everything. I was displaced and imposing my will in every menial part of my day. I exhausted myself. It had been a month of sobriety, and Evelyn's first Christmas became our priority. Little did I know, it would be our only Christmas for many years to come.

Christmas in Thailand can be pretty contrived. There are ornaments hung in mall stores and large trees where foreigners work or gather, but Christmas is forgotten in Thailand after that. It would be impossible to recreate anything close to a New England Christmas, anyway. Getting a little fake tree and ornaments without hooks was hardly anything to celebrate, but we (Annie and I) pretended to live our fabulous lives on social media. We shared publicly the pictures that we took the only time the floor was clean enough or the apartment presentable enough. It looked amazing from nine thousand miles away, I bet. We dressed Evelyn up in a little Santa suit that she loathed and took a few quick photos of her opening gifts, sent mostly by my parents. There was a palpable tension between myself, Annie, and even Yai.

Evelyn was suffering with a cough. We would take her for appointments but there wasn't much any doctor could say that helped. We would give her medicated nebulizers. Our apartment was less than two hundred feet from the highway, and Bangkok was hot, dry, and dusty. I thought logic would help, but apparently Yai's best logical reason for Evelyn's cough was hemorrhagic fever. I had enough of the stupidity and drew the line in the sand. I was going to bring Evelyn to the States whether Yai approved it or not. Don't get me wrong, she is incredibly sweet, but her stupidity tops any virtue she may possess.

With Annie and I lacking any sort of connection, I had been thinking about getting a new place and officially throwing in the marriage towel - not that I hadn't really already done that day in and day out for the entire life we shared in the Philippines. Annie had spoken up and called attention to the elephant in the room that night that Yai and I argued about the best way to treat Evelyn's cough. She suggested that maybe it was time for me to find my own place. I couldn't have agreed more. It had been two months almost since I arrived back on Annie's radar and things were no better. I would bring up moving to the US with Annie only to have it ignored. It was clear from this conversation that as of then we would be co-parenting in Bangkok.

We would rotate days bringing Evelyn to the pool - she was able to swim without floaties at a very young age. She would live in the water if she could. Evelyn was amazed by just about any body of water. It made entertaining her extremely affordable, and that was appreciated as my first consultancy would be ending soon and I would be seeking a new, full-time job, once again, in Bangkok. My face had been printed onto the group's menus, and cardboard cutouts of yours truly could be found in most of the large malls. My consultancy at the very least level of impact has given me some cred in Bangkok. I was struggling with my cravings still, and I could feel the reservations creep in just as the thought of moving materialized. That's where my addiction waited so patiently for his next opportunity.

Annie and I finally acknowledged outwardly that our mutually agreeable separation would be a load off both of us. Annie and Yai both seemed to lighten up. I was told Evelyn could come with me whenever I wanted to get her. I began looking for apartments close to Evelyn's birthday. On March 4, 2012, exactly one year after the most amazing day of my life, Evelyn's birthday, I found a new apartment with Annie's help.

We agreed to take Evelyn to Ocean World to celebrate the best day in all three of our lives. Ocean World is an indoor aquarium in one of the world's most prestigious malls, Siam Paragon. As we paid our deposit at my new apartment and got ourselves ready to head out for Evelyn's birthday, we started to walk down the narrow dirt road that led from my new place to the main street, or pahk soi, as the Thais call it. I was holding a clinging Evelyn in my left arm as we walked down the left side of the alley with her baby bag, our portable changing station, strapped over my right shoulder. Annie was behind me in single file as it was too narrow in the alley to walk side-by-side. As we neared the main road I heard a motorbike coming up on our rear. I gave a glance back to make sure we could all fit. I noticed two guys on a motorbike flying towards us, but recognized we all fit perfectly well with the width of the alley. I started to turn back up the alley to continue walking. When the motorbike had finally caught up to us earlier than I was expecting, I felt a forceful tug. The baby bag was ripped right from my shoulder. Clenching firmly onto Evelyn with protective fury, I realized the motorbike boys had marked us and jacked our bag by design. Normally, Annie and I would have our wallets on us, but because of the intense heat and fact that we would be heading to Ocean World from my place and walking a good deal, we had both emptied our pockets right into the baby bag. All the money we owned was in that bag!

I handed Evelyn to Annie and sprinted up the street. I could still make out the bike when I hurled myself onto the back of taxi bike. The taxi, responsive to my pointing and screaming at the thieves, floored it, and we were in pursuit. The taxi assured me we would stay in sight. We were cruising, and he was hanging with them through the tollways and deceptively sneaky alleys. There were two men. One was a skinny crackhead type, and the other was a fat shit that looked like he had repeatedly mistaken confectioner's sugar for cocaine during a twenty-year binge. He was the one who violated me....us.... on Evelyn's birthday. We were getting close enough to attempt pulling him down, and I had great vision of the road in front of me. My taxi clearly had a better bike, so I went for it. I had the fat guy's T-shirt in my grip, and I saw real panic on his face. As I went to pull back to flip him off his bike and recover my bag, and Evelyn's birthday money, I yanked. I was willing to risk my safety and my new taxi hero's safety for this, clearly. I yanked back with as much force as a guy traveling double on a 100cc motorbike through the crowded streets of Bangkok could yank. I came up with an empty, ripped t-shirt and pulled my taxi into a curb. As we made impact, the bike turned into a human slingshot, hurling me over the handlebars, I could feel the pain of losing this battle more than the road rash. I lost them, and it crushed me. Evelyn's first birthday was ruined.

My first few nights in my new place were lonely ones. I was still fighting the voice in my head imploring me to let him out. He wasn't going away. Days after I lost Evelyn's bag and I moved into my place, I was back on Soi 3 looking for a fix. I hated myself for being there. I told myself to just go home, to cope, deal, exist in the discomfort, but my disease wouldn't let me. To others, it is inconceivable why a struggling addict would put his drug back inside his or her body after any length of time clean, but the disease is never cured. It is arrested by connection and progression. I was no longer connected, my job was ending, and I was going to be broke and unemployed in days, as a father. You'll never hear me excuse myself for anything I've chosen to do. I had been expecting this day to come. Every addict should expect it when they haven't employed a single act of continued sobriety, a responsive dialogue, or efforts to change the guy that left the Philippines some nine months ago.

Time was never on my side, and even less so after Evelyn was born. This every parent knows, but my interpretation of this shrinking vortex of impossibility was unique. I would get high all day and wonder as I was high, "What are my realistic possibilities for the day?" Most tweakers can look out a window for days on end, high on meth, without even a sip of water or morsel of food. The audacity I had to question time after this I find laughable. I estimate less than five percent of my daily plans while I was high got taken care of or followed through. I value congruence but act in contradiction to my integrity whenever I'm high. There is no effort needed to speak, but the drugs made it impossible to act out. All the eye-opening facts in the world wouldn't help an addict. I would have blamed anything other than myself for anything while I was high.

I had time to get Evelyn, and I would every day. I would have no agenda or purpose other than just existing next to her. I would give it all to Evelyn if I could because I just knew there was something in her seemingly contented little face that made our time and connection arbitrarily amazing. She loved me, and she loved her mother and her Yai. I kept Evelyn stimulated and talked to her as I would a shrink. Evelyn started swimming without floaties in April of that year, when she was thirteen months.

Having moved into a new apartment without my next job and lined up and trying to cope with co-parenting in Bangkok, something that wasn't even on the table six months ago, I found myself back to the two grams of meth a day habit I left in the Philippines nine months prior. In nine months I had been pacifying my addiction with addictive behaviors and alternative drugs while briefly back in the States. I never made it back to a comfortable headspace in those nine months. I was just starting to realize how powerful crystal meth is. My days with Evelyn were getting more sporadic. I was behind on rent, again, as was my life standard, after one month. My apartment was shaded and dark. I cranked the air conditioner to "freeze me" and got high daily. My subconscious had decided to self-destruct once again. I admit I could have never seen myself staying in Bangkok then and rebuilding my life as a co-parent while still legally married. I couldn't be sure of who I really was as a father without any family around and a drug habit that was gripping me, eating me from the inside out. The path ahead seemed lonely and so far from what I envisioned a couple years back when Annie told me she was pregnant. Annie was starting to see the addict in me get worse again. I remember getting frisked by police one afternoon at Annie's apartment while picking up Evelyn. Yai's venture into private investigation was taking on more business. The clerk at the front desk in my condo unit had told me there was a female calling to get tabs on who was in my apartment and when. Thais will always share this information with other Thais. I appreciated him giving me the heads up, though. I would notice Yai trailing me as late as one in the morning in red light districts. It was a case Annie was building, and one she didn't need that much effort in figuring out.

Seven weeks after Evelyn's birthday, April 27, 2012, when Evelyn was thirteen months old, Annie would angrily remove Evelyn from a mall in Thong Lor, Bangkok where we were enjoying a day, as we did in our own oblivion. That would be the last time I would see my daughter's face for over three years. There was nothing I could do. Police reports already forbade me to go to Annie's home. I had no money, no job, and a bigger meth habit than at any other point in my existence. Annie was overwhelmed and disgusted with me. She would be fired from that great job I got for her by complaining about my habit while at her job. Things were clear.

Having calls go unanswered from the person that had my child was maddening. Add that along with being high in general and you have the recipe for a suffocating place to live. My head was a mess. I second-guessed everything. Every minute was internally contentious, and any human interaction was a desperate attempt to feel a breath of progression. Then I staggered some more. The cycle is relentless and cruel, but I caused it. I knew that day she was different. Annie, I mean. She was angry and fed up. I understand her anger with our situation, but I was never high with Evelyn. I took care of her as any good dad would. I was perplexed. Annie spoke firmly in our brief history about understanding that Evelyn would need me, and in turn, never remove us from each other's lives. I was naive and had been growing angrier by the day. I was isolated and using to keep my head and anger from committing a grave mistake. I numbed myself. I always found a way to survive.

I went to our great embassy in Bangkok and was turned away by ambassadors reciting The Hague Convention and stating their policy of not interfering in lost children cases unless we could find our way on US soil. The Hague Convention is just a pretentious, post-WWII way the United Nations adopted of validating a country's refusal to honor another country's parent-to-parent kidnapping visas and costs and monitoring. I was lost. I had no money to take Annie to court. I just missed my daughter. Self-loathing was a daily wake up ritual...replacing one high after the next. The next flight home would be at my parents' "I told you so" expense. No one actually thought I would be coming home with my daughter. I was getting known for epic letdowns.

Self-assessment is the toughest form. Everyone sees what we see in ourselves long before we do. I knew I was desperate, but for Evelyn, I always was. I just wanted her to have the life she would want. Thailand was beautiful, but they are third world and subservient by nature. Evelyn was undeniable - both as my child physically and in her young character. She never took no for an answer and could shovel food down like she was packing a dump truck. Both textbook characteristics for a Garon. She has my identical facial contour, eyebrows, eye shape, mouth, and ears. She suffers from the flat Thai nose, however. She has dark brown hair, chipmunk cheeks, a giant toothless smile, and a spirit - a healthy, glowing spirit. She just amazes me.

My last couple months in Bangkok that year were nothing short of horrifying. I was seeing one prostitute that I ordered for a threesome, and eventually took off on without paying, during the last six weeks. I had the audacity to call her again when I got back from yet another visa run. She accepted my invite to make amends for stiffing her, and I was starting to get a bad name at most agencies for nonpayment. I would take whoever was willing at this point. I had a thing for breaking rules, but that mantra burns quite a few bridges. She, my new regular girl, was sweet and logical, and she knew very little English. We got high every time I saw her. She told me how much she loved getting high and also how much she hated getting high. She had a bit of acne from getting high, which I could tell made her slightly uncomfortable. She had thick thighs for a four-foot-ten Thai girl, and she dressed to compliment those thighs. We connected through my blunt honesty about using and giving my child away. Her name was Yui, and I had an instant infatuation with her. She broke her walls down quickly. I needed that vulnerability, especially from a prostitute I had accepted a girlfriend application from. She was round, but very petite and skinny, if that makes sense? Her features were round.

Yui was eighteen when we met on that escort call, and we shared drugs, our story, women, duties, and money. She knew I was poor, but she still enjoyed being with me, even when she heard I would be leaving back to the States soon. Yui and I spent every day together of my last couple months in Bangkok of 2012. We vowed to keep in touch when I left. I told her I would be back for her, and I would. Yui was the distraction I needed to get well enough to get home and reset my plan of chasing my way back to Evelyn.

I landed, once again empty handed, in Boston in late June and immediately had résumés out. I needed to work and make money fast. I grew more and more self-absorbed with being a victim that I forgot I was the villain. I refused to share my part in losing my own child. I reveled in my support through phished out empathy from social media posts and spoke as if I were a martyr for fathers everywhere chasing their paternal rights. I wasn't capable of waking up the day after payday with a penny in my pocket. I had paid no bills for as long as I can remember, and I had no real friends actively involved in my life. The hollow, black-eyed shell of my body floated through days that my astral being decided to run for the hills. I was on a repeat-until-dead cycle of life. Life in my parents' house again was painful and a grim reminder of my failures. I needed to be gone, and the next gig that came calling was getting a chef. That place was Fresh, Ogunquit, Maine, USA.

8 | OGUNQUIT - 2012

The headhunter that sold me on this job was intent that if it were agreeable to the owners that it be contract, short term, and seasonal, I could be heading back to Bangkok in a few months to fulfill my plan of getting a top notch lawyer and pleading it out in court for custody of Evelyn. At the very least, I figured I would be getting time back with Evelyn this way. I had emails to four or five law firms regarding my divorce/custody bullshit. I heard back from two, and the one I chose… I never sent a dime. Meth was still not prevalent on the East Coast of the US, but I, once again, was accepting any attempted replacement I could get my hands on. I spent the first three days of that contract working two consecutive forty-one-hour shifts with a five-hour nap thrown in. The hiring group, whose business name was Three Fags and a Hag, was looking to get a shell of a hollowed out gas station turned into a full service, fast casual, patisserie style grab and go restaurant in seventy-two hours. They were pressed to be open by the Fourth of July, which in the US, in a seasonal city, is of paramount importance to business revenue. I was awarded the contract because I promised a soup to nuts restaurant opening in three days. I started July 1st and was told to be open with the full menu available by July 4th. There wasn't a piece of small ware nor utensil nor appliance. It was hollow. I had no limit to what I thought I could do and occasionally impressed myself. We opened at six in the morning on July 4th. I was on fumes having worked eighty-two of the previous eighty-seven hours, but I felt good. I would email Annie every day that summer. Some emails were lengthy and threatening, some short and concise. I was as unstable as my written dialogue depicted. I could always smooth talk, high or not.

Yui and I would Skype every day. I knew she was still turning tricks in Bangkok, but I had other problems to sort out. I enjoyed her company, even on Skype. My living situation, as my new employers were offering accommodation in this high energy, eighty percent gay community, was above the diner the group owned and directly across the street from my restaurant/patisserie. It made my life a lot easier, but it was also easier to get high.

As I began recruiting staff, I was met with a slew of foreigners on J1 visas. The town was so drastically seasonal that it required short-term staff. I was fonder of foreigners and still am. I find all classes of American culture still lacking the ability to offer time and be wrong. Two things I grew to value over all else. My roommates were two Turkish busboys and a Jamaican busboy, Damien. They worked for the same owners that I did, just at a busier restaurant down the cove. The busboy trio would eat off the customers' uneaten meals throughout the day and bake one potato when they got home each night. They lived simply, and I would look forward to getting home and talking about our days while smoking weed with Damien as the Turkish brothers scrunched their disapproving noses. I was exhausted trying to keep up with Fresh, my new work baby. We would reconvene back above Bessie's, the diner we lived over, and talk about our days. I was starting to hire - three gay bartenders from one of the managing partner's staffs at his gay bar, Maine Street, and two Romanians - one guy and one girl. Ioana, the female, and I would go on to have a real friendship. I can't say it was a really real - we were attracted to each other but being twelve years apart in age really tested her integrity and called her true self onto the proverbial floor. I spent as many nights as I could at the gay bar with my gay security boys that were dually employed at the gay bar and Fresh turning down aggressive, homosexual advances, because Ioana felt like hanging out there. There wasn't much nightlife in the quaint, predominantly gay community of Ogunquit. I enjoyed it to some degree, but I could never be a regular.

As time when on, I was offered the opportunity to work at the gay bar once Fresh closed up at eight in the evening and moonlight while serving shots in my tightey-whitey underwear for an extra five hundred dollars a night. Being pressed for lawyer money and having accumulated nothing in my first three weeks, I went for it. Gay men always had a thing for me. Working in restaurants, I was often heckled and made uncomfortable by the abundance of overly aggressive gay men. It didn't bother me anymore. I accepted advances for tips, and I played the role well. I had no shame in the things I did or needed to do. It's as if I wasn't born with that gene. I wouldn't even know where I could buy some shame. I was weeks from my thirty-third birthday - living above a breakfast diner with three immigrants, buying molly (MDMA), weed, and pills from random local inbred teenagers, Skyping my prostitute girlfriend back in Bangkok, and thinking life was just splendid. I was losing my drive to get back to Evelyn through numbing my feelings. I hated myself for it, but I would have killed myself then if I left myself alone with those thoughts. 'the other guy' was the only way I made it back to Bangkok still breathing.

August of 2012 saw my summer and contract in Ogunquit winding to a close. I was about to turn thirty-three. I was living above a breakfast diner with three immigrants, buying dime bags of weed, grams of molly, taking psychedelic mushrooms, working nights at the gay bar in my underwear for cash tips, and taking care of my prostitute girlfriend in Bangkok. I had dabbled in heterosexual still porn a bit at the request of some of the gay men. Life on paper wasn't nearly as awful as it appeared, or so I thought. By now, thoughts of Evelyn were as strong as day one, but I numbed my opportunity to take better care of my addiction. I replaced one fix after another. I was incapable of living a normal life. I accepted this....

Yui was clamoring for me to get back to Bangkok, and I convinced myself that proximity to Evelyn, however I managed to get back, was going to be how I pressured Annie into letting me see her. I wanted to see if Yui was still escorting too, so in spite of her saying that she was not accepting Johns, I decided to book her services through her agency and see if she would accept my booking as I made it under a fake name, Gino Valentine. Yui promptly accepted the booking, as per my conversations through email with her pimp or mamasan confirming her arrival. After calling Yui to the floor on this and sending her my proof, she caved. She swore off escorting that day and assured every fiber of my soul she was going to be faithful. I accepted her apology and continued to follow through with my plans on heading back. To this day I am certain Yui has never escorted again. If, at the very least, I could have saved something to build on from my level of dark and evil, this was the meniscus of a silver lining.

My emails and Western Union transfers throughout the summer to Annie went unanswered, and the money was never picked up. Ioana and I would say our awkward goodbyes, as I would with the gay boys. I had grown a bond with several of them that summer, and I shared a last fun night. I ultimately, at their request, sent a spread of nudes of myself to their phone numbers as I drove off to the airport in early September. I would get sporadic texts that just said, "thank you," with a splash emoji. The splash emoji was the one context clue that summed up the thank you. I had helped relieve some gay sexual tensions that summer without having to give up my ass. I always say, "Better to work towards the solution than to get stuck on the problem." Those guys were good to me that summer, so I repaid my gratitude.

9 | KOH PHANGAN - 2013

I arrived back in Bangkok five months from my last correspondence with Annie or Evelyn in September of 2012. I was looking for work, but my interests were from groups of restaurants that needed me to be in Bangkok before expressing their interest in interviewing me. My trip out was hugely contested by my family. They saw a guy chasing his next high and adventure, and certainly not one buckling down and asserting himself into a legal, rightful custody battle to get his child back that he obnoxiously claimed to need. They were right, but my addiction didn't give a fuck. I needed more of whatever worked best in taking my mind off Evelyn. Meth was my need. It never goes away. It lurks, as I said, for the day it catches a glimmer of hope. Bangkok was the world's greatest playground for my addiction, and I knew this. I lied to myself…well, 'the other guy' lied to myself, and I believed it all.

Yui met me at the airport - we would be staying at her family's shophouse in Klong Toey, Bangkok, a poor community in a booming metropolis, and we fit the spec. We had nothing. I used the rest of whatever I had left after the flight and travel costs for a bag of meth and a taxi home. We would play online poker, beg for scraps of food, and wait in the shophouse until the government cut our electricity. We ate mama noodles when we found some scratch to eat, but mostly we just accrued a tab at the food hawkers down on the street. Yui would beg for the two of us. I loved her for this. The Thai people in that neighborhood kept me alive for the first couple months until I found work. We eventually had our electricity cut for nonpayment. The shophouse next to ours was willing to let us run an extension cord so we could use a fan and computer. The fan was to stay alive in the burning heat while the computer was our lifeline to the outside world of gainful employment. I sent out résumés, called contacts, and even submitted applications through chat bubbles and reservation requests. I was not giving up. Yui and I were trying to live healthily in spite of forming this love from a common toxic bond that was overrun with the illegal sex trade and methamphetamines. We acted out of love for one another in spite of our matching addictions. Yui did better at it than I did. I snuck bags when I could. My addiction wouldn't let go that easily.

I received an email about a week into our pirated electrical situation asking me if I felt comfortable acting as chef and general manager of a boutique resort set to open December 26, 2012. It was now mid-October, and I needed work. I had been passed over on two other positions in Bangkok and Phuket, so the urgency to find employment was at a high. I accepted the offer and planned to assume the lead role in all things pertained to operating Kuupoo Kuupoo - Koh Phangan. I had been to Koh Phangan a couple times as it was the universally known land of full moon party and half moon party - scandalous beach parties that attracted men and women from all walks to the beaches of Haad Rin, Koh Phangan for hedonistic celebrations and glow-in-the-dark fantasies fulfilled. Yui agreed to come with me and help wherever she could. She was in love, and I was taken with her commitment to being clean and living a normal life. Normal life, I say, but that is in direct correlation to the environment and culture we were subject to. This is what attracted me to Thai people - congruence and fortitude.

Yui and I set out on a tour bus to Koh Phangan as directed by the French owner, Patrice. Patrice was a sly old dog with a steady pulse on his businesses and less empathy than yours truly. I loved his style. He had already opened two very successful locations of Kuupoo Kuupoo in Bali, Indonesia. He had originally bought two hotels in 2002 in Bali, only to have the island bombed in 2003. This stagnated the tourism the island thrived off of and Patrice, being only a real estate magnate at the time, opted to employ personnel to launch the hotels back into full operations. Bali was a beautiful place. The soil is volcanic, as there is an active volcano on the island. There are beautiful beaches and unmatched sunsets. Surfers were rich in abundance, as were the mellow vibes in the beaches of Semenyak and Kata. Rice paddies flowed down the cliffs of luscious green mountains as trains chugged up the hills to get to the cultural center of Bali, Ubud. Pigs were openly roasted and there was a soccer field right in the heart of the center. Shophouses were full of unearthed art and worldly talents. It wasn't long before Patrice had success as a hotelier. The island couldn't stave off tourism if it tried, because that plan had already failed.

Patrice ventured onto Koh Phangan in search of a place to open his third hotel. The beach land he purchased was insanely beautiful. There was one giant rock you could swim out to and get soft shell crabs for dinner and see a sunset that had no rival. His taste was impeccable; plush king beds under forty-foot teakwood peak ceilings with open concept ceramic tub baths, fancy foot benches, mosquito nets draped from the ceiling encasing the bed, infinity pools on the deck of every villa, Koi ponds in our front office, and the most elegant wedding packages on earth.

I arrived on the heavily mafia-controlled island on October 26th, 2012. Exactly two months prior to opening. Walking up to the front steps would have been nice, but what I walked up to was a mudslide and what looked like an abandoned hillside with squatters taking up the leftover shelter. October and November were notoriously wet with flash floods being the catch of the day. There was an empty infinity pool extending the full length of the resort with several half-finished beach villas on the beach level. There were water tanks that looked to be broken walkways filled the jungle level villa paths, and the jungle level villas were still, after over two years of construction, nothing more than a pile of wood.

Lionel, a Frenchman, greeted me with a warm smile. It's hard not to find the overdressed white guy in Thailand. He had been living on the island for the past year with no family or friends, overseeing and directing a team of Thai engineers at the mercy of delivery sea cargo containers dropped off regularly over the course of three years, all which contained a connect-by-number replication of the Bali hotels. Lionel was under-qualified and overmatched for the project. He spoke no Thai, making even more difficult an already near impossible project with an even more unreachable deadline. There was wood and partially complete concrete mixes all around, containers of linens and spa materials unopened and stuffed into small office closets buried in the hillside behind the villas, farthest from the sea. The entire place was disregarded and understaffed for completion. Functioning high on meth every day was never an issue for me. I jumped in headfirst at Kuupoo Kuupoo.

I made myself fancy business cards and cleared out an office. I still have one of those fancy cards. I got to work on inputting every piece of small ware and operating equipment I could. I reached out to other GMs I knew from Koh Samui about front office software, technicians, tailors, wedding planners, recruiters, Burmese laborers, air-condition techs, generators, blueprints, and several other "everythings" that go into being the sole operator of a five-star hotel set to open in six weeks with about a twenty-five percent completion rate. I was fucked. Lionel was set to leave the next day, turning the property over to me. Yui worked by my side every day, always eager to be of help. She saved my ass. She worked on the phones to expedite my shitty Thai conversations that sometimes led to way more effort than was needed. She was a beast for me.

Yui didn't know that I was using still. I mean, she did, obviously, but she did very well at hiding it. Meth turns me into a different human. I can't fucking stand that guy, as I've said. The effect does keep me focused in my work, but it leaves everyone around me feeling uneasy about life in general, being led by some overpaid, foreign tweaker. I carry on as I would, regardless.

The engineers had been there for three years and in the blink of an eye, some foul-mouthed drug head with a build comes in and starts ripping through everything. I got it. I totally got it. Didn't change my objective, nonetheless.

I always felt comfortable being in charge, high on meth or not. I made good company decisions and what I lacked for in experience, I made up for in sweat ethic. I worked hard, I expected a lot, and I tried to give back more than I would ever expect. This made some Thais follow me hard. This made others insecure about their own ability to keep up. I got that too. I am and always have been, without argument, an acquired taste.

This crew was tough, but they were divided, and I could feel it from the beginning. Two couples, families with children were one half of the divide. They were the resentful group. Their efforts never seemed to be appreciated enough. The group seemed to have two leaders. The head of that family-based group was Sakhon, a young, resourceful Thai engineer. He was polite, but I would hear about how he spoke about me from several others, including some of his devout accomplices. His wife and their two children occupied the apartment that was first finished, an obvious sign that, at one point, he had been the head of this entire group. Sakhon was rebellious by nature, and we would bump heads quite often. Looking at things with compassion was new to me, but I did empathize with him having a family and being a good provider and father. I wanted the staff to work towards a greater good. He was on board.

Mon, a middle-aged Thai man with a hang-dog jowl was the elder of the staff. He seemed to have gained the respect and right to lead over time. Mon was a soft-spoken, humble man with a fearful disposition toward foreigners. I could tell his English was nil and his experience with foreigners was less, if that's possible. He seemed at peace when the rest of the staff was frantic. The whole staff had finished three villas in total, to the best of their ability, with six weeks to opening. We needed to get nine of the twenty villas ready to handle our bookings until the new year. By the second week of January we would need to have three more finished, including the rope walkways over the water tanks. The resort owner Patrice and his IT guy, Laurent, thought they should take reservations the year before, not knowing when the resort would be finished. Things were tense for good reason. As the next couple weeks went by the engineers and I worked around the clock, ate together, emptied every dropped off container together, and made a resort into a family clubhouse. Life was getting good again, and I was happy. For those six weeks spent pre-opening we had a lot of fun, but a lot of rain, as it was also two months of one of the worst rainy seasons Thailand had in years. We worked through mudslides, missed deliveries, government electricity rations, monitor lizard forced evictions, dangerous snakes, and some seriously nasty geckos. They, the Geckos, look so tranquil stuck upside down on the wall, just until they scamper towards your face with jagged, demon-like teeth and your engineer has to rescue you from your own bitch-like screaming.

I was paused in my drug use for a spell and would wait until I had a day to rest. The resort completion was something even my addiction prioritized. Even 'the other guy' knew we were running short on options if we lost this one. I would be as low profile as a big-mouthed dickhead could be. I would find a girly bar on the island, rent a girl or two, have them connect with their dealer, and go back to setting up the resort when we had our short time fun. Yui was left back at our new treetop villa, which we moved into as was part of my contract, to sit anxiously waiting and knowing what I was up to. It would take a couple more years before I grew any relationship integrity.

Yui, as far as I was concerned in my toxic addictive mind, owed me her life. It was she that actually was rescuing me. Without her drive to stay clean, I wouldn't have had any sober stretches. I tried to make her happy, but I knew our romance would eventually dissolve. She and I had an understanding that we were helping each other through the other's transition. Mine into resort manager and aspiring father, hers as a non-prostitute and gainfully employed Thai citizen. We used each other with mutual consent.

I went through interviews for spa therapists, front office staff, housekeeping, kitchen, service staff, IT, finance, and then right into software for hotel and resort management. I hired every position needed in a two-week span. Everyone, all thirty or so people, including two French spies who were sent by Patrice to observe my progress, worked twelve-to-fifteen-hour days for two weeks leading up to opening. Sunny, my acquaintance whom I recruited knowing she was out of work, was experienced in a front office setting. She spoke English, and was living just next door in Koh Samui, our mother island and my former home. She was an important teammate going down the stretch. I sent her to Samui for the last plush mattress that I knew of existing in Thailand. It was a bit of overkill, but after our deliveries shorted us the night before our first guests arrived, she was my hero. She made the last ferry with a king-sized mattress on board. We were set to open.

Leading up to the opening day, the Burmese staff, who Thais

viewed as lesser beings, was up in the forty-foot villa rafters wiping the ceilings, hanging the mosquito nets, and polishing the pool deck. The Thai staff was preparing our last meal together before we opened. The front office staff was racing around the island to pick up the uniforms we had had tailored. Everyone was harmonious. I was amazed and grateful for every ounce of work we all put into the arrival of Kuupoo Kuupoo.

Kuupoo Kuupoo, through the hard work of the opening team, myself, and Yui, opened to a five-star rating with most Internet portals, including Trip Advisor. I was immediately interviewed by the Condé Nast Traveler, and the New York Times ranked us as the world's thirty-first top destination in 2013.

The problem with success, for me, was the shitshow that usually followed. It was coming. As the resort maintained well above average low season capacity and smashed expectations, I began to pat myself on the back again. My back pats were usually paid in crystal meth followed by epic fallout and horror. Evelyn was still missing her dad. I was still excluded from her life. My fifty plus emails were disregarded and not answered. My pain was back. I should have been equipped by this point to say "no." I wasn't…I don't know if meth is ever something I won't taste.

As the resort flourished, I floundered. I started to accumulate my usual round of hoes, and not the garden variety. I had a plug for meth set up, so off running I went. I would have multiple villas set up for more drug-induced fantasies while my daughter was somewhere I knew not of. This saddens me still.

The lawyer for the resort and woman responsible for all visas, social security, business licensing, and other legal matters, was an affluent member and mafia named Sopha. She and I would never once agree in my time running Kuupoo Kuupoo. She was a very tall, black-skinned Thai woman, heavyset with dreads and lots of yellow gold jewelry. Sopha knew of what I did in my spare time and that I was illegally hiring cheaper Burmese workers ahead of Thais. She had a deep tone of contention every time we spoke. Once the resort was open and I was back to the trash bag version of myself, Sopha would grow leerier of my purpose and compliance with life in general. She detested me, and she wasn't someone a foreigner should be looking to upset.

I had hired qualified accountants, and they held me accountable. Sakhon and Mon had started working together and eating together. I encouraged and convinced Patrice to allocate money to support staff housing. Everyone was happy. Patrice had gained clearance to fly in early February, and we were all excited to meet the guy signing our paychecks.

Patrice arrived the day after Valentines Day. He was impressed. He told me when they hired me that they gave me a five to ten percent chance of getting open. I thought this was pretty funny, because I gave myself less. He appreciated me, and I enjoyed our time together. Patrice knew about the discord between the engineering team. We stayed in close communication up until opening regarding construction standards, but since opening two months ago, the engineers had settled their differences, but not with Patrice, apparently. Sakhon and Patrice had some bad air. Allegedly, there was an agreement that Sakhon lived in the hotel apartment only until the resort opened. I had not heard about this, but then again, it was none of my business.

Patrice offered his wisdom and applauded my intelligence. We set up filtration for the koi pond and the couples' dining gazebo. We stayed with each other his whole trip. He knew there was some darkness about me, but he would always assume it was a gambling vice. I had that one too, but it's down the list. Getting ready to see Patrice off to the ferry, he said he had to speak with me. I wasn't prepared for what he wanted. He gave me no chance for rebuttal; it was clear, I had to fire Sakhon. I was opposed to it, but I followed through. I asked him to leave after three years of building the resort out of a mud pile, send his son and daughter away homeless, his wife angered, and myself with no out for his recourse. It crushed me and the spirit we filled the resort with. Sakhon, in our minds, had repaid his indignation and redeemed himself. He was a part of our family, and he didn't take it well.

Yui had been working in the kitchen as a salaried worker, and we were doing ok outside of my weekly excursions to get drugs and hookers. I got her a white Chihuahua. She named him "Look-Chin," which means "baby piece." I figured Look -Chin would keep Yui happy, or at least distracted, while I was out ripping up the island. She was the only person to know before Sakhon knew about his pending release, and even she begged me not to. I regret not standing up to Patrice, but it was his resort. Sakhon would launch an attack back at the resort out of spite. My plumbing pipes were cut, generator sabotaged, snakes were in villas, and monitor lizards were now living under two villas, making it Look-Chin who should now have to worry. Sakhon was sabotaging the resort after lost face in the embarrassment of his firing, the worst thing you can do to a Thai. I separated him from his work family and sent his real family away without a home. I struggled internally. He wasn't deserving of it, and now we had to bear the brunt of his butt sore feelings.

Evelyn's second birthday. I went shopping over in Koh Samui after taking the ferry to shop for gifts. It had been more than ten months since I saw her last. I wondered about what she looked like now and if she had any recollection of me. I knew she hadn't, but I pretended. It helped me feel better. I bought her a knockoff Burberry jumper, a book, and a dinosaur toy. I had always been financially running on empty thanks to a massive drug habit. I was ashamed at having less than an adequate bankroll to get Evelyn something nice. I still did my best with a hole and giant, obvious missing piece in my heart. I mailed Evelyn's birthday gift to the address I had for Annie, but the package was undeliverable. I continued emailing in hopes of getting a response. That response was still years away.

April came and Thai New Year. Songkran had quickly become my favorite holiday. It was a one-week water fight between any smiling face and the next. Thais and foreigners all had a blast during Songkran. Thais would run up and pat baby powder on passersby's faces as they got splashed by Super Soakers and water pails. The whole country stopped and celebrated. There were no TV ads or companies looking to profit off the holiday. It was pure, organic happiness. It was at the end of the week of fun and festivities that the country gathered itself and moved forward through another year. In Koh Phangan, it was only a matter of seeing through the holiday until Sopha set her plan into action. I was her target.

After having the resort running at max capacity and one happy guest after the next and even catering an entire beach wedding laced with exotic flowers, elephants, fireworks, and honeymoon packages that included embroidered robes and couples massages, Sopha was reportedly irate at the fact that I had not yet applied for the Thai national's Social Security or gone to renew my own visa, and that I was a class A meth-head running his mouth and money at most of the islands known girly bars. As I said, I stopped going to her pointless meetings. I was overdue for a visit.

My visit came with a stroke of circumstantial luck. It was a hot morning in April, and I had just finished procuring a teak boat for island tours and adding hotel owned motorbikes for rental. We were growing fast, but Sopha was resolved in her mind as to what should come of me. That hot Sunday morning an armed goon with a pistol was creeping down the walkway towards the treetops where my villa was when my Assistant GM, Snek, encountered the man and asked his purpose. The gentleman explained in Thai that he was instructed to shoot me in the head and harm no one else. He appeared a little wobbly. Sopha had had enough of my arrogance and mansplaining. I had enough drugs, girls, and misery to want it to all be over, but Snek saved me. He grabbed all the money he could from the front office and offered it to the man for a few minutes that he might drive around the block and come back. The goon obliged. He must have owed Sopha a favor, because he settled for a small take. Snek sent the housekeeping attendant to fetch me in my villa. Zen, the attendant, interrupted Yui and I engaged in some morning doggie fun, but we paused, blue balls and all, to get the fuck on the teak boat and off the island. Patrice had been sending me warning emails, but my notifications were off, and they went unanswered. Yui and I saw the goon re-entering the resort as we boarded the boat. He looked like he spent the previous eight hours on a bar stool coming to grips with his upcoming task. Patrice had sent a boat to Koh Samui to get me and take me to Bali, but I was in no shape or head space to be jumping countries again and running from my most important duties - those of a father.

I would go back to Bangkok to take Yui home and then return myself back to the US. There was a little problem, however. I was on an overstay from not having my tourist visa renewed. I was an illegal immigrant, essentially. I would need, at the very least, seven hundred dollars to pay my overstay, I had no money, and my family was close to done with me. I was run down and ragged.

Drugs, as I have been saying all along, take everything. They took every last friend and the hope they may have once had in me. They take our insides without me knowing and expose our deepest fear. They cut through our character, leaving no trace of the human we are looking for. They take positive change and trust. They take the people we need, and I ruin them again when my addiction resurfaces. They take my pride and valor, patience, and resourcefulness. They take me to a person that needs no introduction by now, but someone I wish to avoid at all costs. They take me.

Yui was put on a train down south to stay with her mom while I went back to that little, run down, quasi-condemned shophouse to stay out my last few days that I would ever live as a Thai resident. I was sick. Soi 3 called my name, and I answered the call. I was messaging friends through social media for money, emailing my brother with stories of tough luck hardship. As I said, self-assessment is the toughest. I would maintain my stance through every lie. It was embarrassing looking back, but I earned the isolation at the time. I wouldn't have dealt with or believed me either. My mother was torn. She knew I had to get home. She would send me money behind my father's (who was definitely done with me by now) back and tell me to get my ass on my flight. She bought me a plane ticket. This was the first time in the five years since I first touched down in Singapore in 2008 that the forecast had no plan B, no bridges left intact, and no people to hear my empty words. Evelyn was two years old now. I was a terrible father up until this point, but it didn't mean I always had to be.

Leaving Bangkok was the biggest struggle my addiction has ever known. I blew the money my mother sent, or should I say, 'the other guy' did. I was always chasing the feeling of the first high, and I never once got there again. I justified my inexcusable acts with my presumptive, cunt-like whining about how I "needed" one last night to go home without a reservation in my mind. It was my addiction negotiating his capture. He was fucked, and I was forcing him into an ultimatum. Knowing that there was never going to be an endless, unquestioned stream of money sent to me, and that all of my nine lives were coming to an end, my addiction pushed back hard. I remember not wanting anything to do with meth, but with a pocket full of cash and a head in chaos, I chose to feed my demon.

Going back to explain what I had done with my mother's money was one of the hardest talks I ever had, even while numb on drugs. I sympathized with my mother's years of agony while I was struggling across the world. My addiction didn't give a fuck, so he made me ask for more. My mother, in tears, agreed with the caveat that it was indefinitely the last time money would be sent. There are no chaperone services for incapacitated adults. I was going to be left to my own free will, which had a track record of epic failure, once again. If I didn't pay this overstay and fee for changing my plane ticket, I would be stuck in Thailand until I could make some money and get back there on my own, and that was a realistic sixty-to-ninety-day plan.

I had gone to pick up the money with twenty-eight hours before my flight boarded. The fact that I had only time to burn with an eye on my hopeful freedom from meth should speak volumes as to the actual volume of the voice in my head telling me everything would be fine, even if we went and blew this wad too. He made me feel as if there wasn't any bridge I couldn't rebuild. He even offered to help. He waits for his moment; he's smarter than me sometimes. His code of ethics is inconceivably minuscule and can be written in one swipe, N/A. They weren't part of his vocabulary.

I forced myself to the airport to lay across a row of steel benches in a far wing of arrivals. I waited, grinding my teeth, palms sweating, and money rubbing against my leg while withdrawing for twenty-eight hours. I felt a sense of accomplishment when the next day came, and I hadn't left the airport. Again, not the stuff one would be hoping to celebrate at thirty-three years old, but it was a catalyst for my next phase of life. I went through security and was brought into immigration once again. Seeing how messy my passport was with all the ins and outs, the officer reviewing my stamps and overstay was eager to get me out of his hair, accept my maximum fine, and stamp me out of Thailand. I was free. It was April 14th, 2013, and I was set to land in Boston. April 15th, the day I landed, happened to be the day of the Boston Marathon bombings. If you're reading this and have no idea what I'm referring to, Google it. The airport was a total scene, police were on high alert, citizens were being searched and violated. It was the home I was geographically born into, so I felt it inherently. I had no idea this was going on. It was a real-life reminder that the world is bigger than me and my problems. As awful as this may be to admit, the destruction caused that day, and the effects of its immediate aftermath were also catalysts for my change.

10 | SALEM, NH - 2014

I was no longer at the mercy of an addict's mindless minutia searching for an out to my jonesing or production to my high. I had been home - living with my family, in Salem, NH, about thirty minutes north of Boston, and living a straight life. I had white knuckled the worst of it, and my withdrawals were subsiding. I started to plan life with Evelyn, even though we were now strangers. It's a strange feeling, acting on blind faith and knowing the outcome will be the right one. Right actions breed right actions. The Tao, a Chinese religion, was my guide and the universe was becoming my God. The cosmic system of weights and balances had been watching me, as they do everyone. My penance was fierce for a man who's never accepted a "no" from anyone. My family was slowly coming around to see bits and pieces of the man they once wished well on his maiden voyage to Singapore with the world at his beck and call and a potential wife in the waiting. They saw progress and accepted my position in the world as being out of their hands. This is what frees an addict's sense of emotional, financial, or monetary debt.

I will wake up tomorrow an addict and every day then on, until I'm dust. There is a real danger in not knowing myself well enough in any given situation, and more so when I'm unaware I need the knowledge. This made me angry on my worst days and grateful and fortuitous on my better days. I refrain from saying best, because in the eyes of any clean addict, including myself, the best days are yet to come. I leant on the Tao for guidance in making decisions - active and non-active. I still believed in Jesus Christ, Mohammed, and Buddha. I am free to believe what I want, so I do. I don't push my beliefs, but I offer anyone that asks a solid explanation. There is certainly a creator and a scientific anomaly to creation. We have so much of our own worldly secrets left to uncover, yet we are off exploring others. I stand by believing that just because we have the power to do something doesn't mean we have to. I am pro-life and non-political because my beliefs venture into those of all sides, predicated on my own logic and integrity. I believe that there is an equal and opposite reaction to our thoughts, our vindictiveness, our intentions, and our actions. I believe we are ultimately, in our creator's version and vision of a way, culpable for how we live our lives and the integrity we act upon. The jackpot will always be sustained happiness. "The happiness that we receive is in direct proportion to the love that we give." - Oprah Winfrey

I was hitting AA meetings, accumulating money, earning friends, and even got me a real girlfriend. Monica McLivingston, a pretty

Irish girl three years my junior, came into my life in late August of 2013, just after my fourth consecutive month of sobriety. I was a fast healer, but I was honest about needing to continue healing, and cautioned myself to the thought of getting too well too fast. Monica and I had a contrived first date, but that was the only thing contrived in our bond. She was a call representative for the country's largest cable provider, and she was very good at her job. She walked with swag and talked with even more confidence. She commanded a level of high integrity and respect. I saw the person in Monica that I wanted to be; she would teach me the difference in my social and intimate levels of integrity. She explained that at a certain point we stop trying to do what we're doing for everyone else and start doing them because it's congruent to the human we know is inside us. I got it. She had what I wanted. Peace of mind and no one to apologize to, no one to overthink the last conversation, no one to pay circumstantial respect towards. She taught me how to be the architect of my own life. Once I got past the shock in the reality that I had none of these essential tools, I followed.

I followed hard; she broke me, and I loved it. My idea of relationship integrity was to just never get caught in any shenanigans. Monica showed me, through her own experiences, how to approach the reality of circumstance and opportunity and accept the flaws of others. She had only one flaw that I could see, and that was inexcusable pride. I was her calm as she was mine. We repaid the gifts we got in the comfort of being able to be our authentic selves, without apology. We would keep each other right sized and pay forward, without the perpetually exhausting need for, the unspoken transparencies a partner would want. She taught me the nuances of avoiding the female wrath. I would walk closest to the road when we were out, sleep closest to the door, buy jewelry and flowers for no reason other than I loved her and wanted her to know. I found myself respecting a human within the boundaries of an intimate relationship for the first time in my life. I wanted to go home to her, and she loved having me there.

I told her about me without euphemisms or sugar-coated bullshit. That alone is enough for most potential girlfriend applicants to withdraw said application. I talked about Evelyn. By now, my moles had been digging through social media to try to tap into Evelyn's life through Annie's profile. There was little to speak of, but every few months a photo or two would surface. The impact a photo has can never trump what seeing her growing face did to me through sporadic photos. I maintained my path in sobriety.

I began working in corporate dining settings for a global corporation. I was starting to comply with our cosmic god's plan for me. Right action breeds right consequence. I felt the happiness of home and balanced it with a manageable workload. I started playing sports again competitively. Pitching and playing baseball were always big parts of my authentic life. I was a fierce competitor. Monica enjoyed this about me, except when we were playing anything against each other. Monica's playful challenge on our first date culminated in her getting my initials tattooed on her ankle. She learned quickly - I hated losing.

Evelyn's life and custody was never a game. I accepted my role in her life as it stood. I caused her position and agreed with Annie. I just wanted to tell her. I wanted to give up my jaded stance for Evelyn to have an opportunity to know me and have the benefits living in the US had to offer over Thailand...not that I was opposed to either. I was woven into the fiber of who I was becoming and loving it. I knew it would take time and faith, both of which I had in abundance.

Monica's daughter, Marley, had a big part in my being well. She was a portly eighth grader when we met, yet I stayed teachable in spite of her age and found the person I would hope that Evelyn would grow into. She said good morning and goodnight and goodbye when she went out. I reciprocated her mindfulness. She treated me as I did her, an equal. We respected each other and accepted the hardships that one might anticipate in step-parenting. I was never her stepdad, but a friend. She and I found a common bond in Marvel comics and poking good fun at Monica, which Monica was very good about taking on the chin. We were a team...no, a family. All three of us. She taught me what I would want and expect out of Evelyn - simply the ability to look any human on earth in the eye and give them an honest response. Simple, yet we as humans struggle with this as technology pushes us further apart as a species.

As time went on, we found a quaint, open concept home overlooking a small private lake in Salem, NH. I played house well; I did all the trash, yard maintenance, handy shit, any heavy lifting, food shopping, and obviously all the cooking. Monica, to her own admission, was a horrible cook. As time and fortified stability rolled on, I still maintained my place in the world as a dad. I was strong and clean. I had a job for over a year, and my rent was paid. I put in the work, and I received the gift of a lifetime.

July 16th, 2015 - I received a reply from Annie to my March 3rd, 2015 email wishing Evelyn a happy fourth birthday:

"Yes, the agreement is you can come to visit Eve here in Thailand and I will send you a video or photo update monthly. You can also Skype with her. For Eve going to US visit her grandparents wait until she turn 18th. About money to support Eve, it's up to your financial. We can have bank account in Eve 's name that u can put money in until she turn 18th then she can get that money or u would like to support her school. Now she is in bi-language school cost 130000 baht/year - she can speak English, not pretty well but better than normal Thai people. Please don't move to Thailand. It's not a good idea for u. I really hope we can work it out. – Annie"

Her English was good enough for me to know the

opportunity I had been waiting over three years for was finally here.

This email arrived three years, two months, and twenty-one days since I last saw Evelyn, Annie, or even heard from either. My email to her was dated March 3rd, 2015:

"Hi Annie,

I just want to wish my daughter a happy birthday. I am not really sure why you stop picking my money up before, but I would really like to work something out.

I really must support her even if you will not let me see her. I know you are happy, and I am happy as well. I just miss her.

I would be willing to give you the divorce you want but I need to see Evelyn sometimes. I have 5 weeks holiday each year from my job and I would like to be able to come visit Evelyn. I do not want to take her away from you ever... I just want to be able to know her. Please tell me what you think and what I can do?

Thank you,
Matt"

I can feel my pain when I read how desperate I was. It makes me second guess every stage of clarity I enter or exist in. All of this meant little as I had the feeling of rebirth. It was the second-best day of my life. Annie and I exchanged emails for a couple hours. Annie had met an Austrian chef, Wally, and had another child, Lea, Evelyn's half-sister. Lea was autistic, which I found odd, because when I asked for Evelyn to be tested for birth defects, the doctor in Thailand told me not to waste my money as those afflictions are far less common in Asian genetics. Wally was Evelyn's step-in for a father. I didn't care to know him, but there was an insane amount of jealousy from Wally towards my being involved with my own daughter. Wally felt so compelled to mask his own insecurities that he sent me a childish message over social media in broken English. I had no problem punching anyone of any size in any place, so I just stuck that one in the memory bank for the opportunity to come. I was all set with knowing him, as I said.

I told Annie about life with Monica and that work was steady for the first time in a while. It was steady for the first time ever, actually. We all agreed life was slow for me and that was a good thing. It was the only thing then. She seemed content with the dialogue enough to confirm that I could chat with Evelyn on Skype the next morning on her way to school, which was twelve hours ahead of us, making it my night before. I would have been more comfortable talking to the pope in a brothel than I felt anticipating seeing and talking to Evelyn for the first time in over three years. I had been sober for just over two years. I was ready to be a father in the worst way, but more nervous about it than I ever had been about anything. Evelyn's existence leveled me, but I was ready to man up.

Annie sent me a warning email just before I signed into Skype. She told me Evelyn spoke only Thai and that she doesn't know who I am, just that she is having a call with a friend of mommies. This crushed me, but time and time again Evelyn nails my ass out of self-destruction.

I hit send on the call. No answer. I could hear my heartbeat and could squeegee the sweat off my hands. Within seconds they were calling back, and when the screen opened, four-year-old Evelyn was looking back at me. My brain couldn't retain a word of that conversation. I was in shock. My smile was unbreakable seeing that kid's face. She was shy and unsure, I thought, as to why she had to talk to me about anything, never mind nothing. It was less than a three-minute call as they were pulling up to Evelyn's kindergarten. I was ok with this. As I sat there reveling in my happiness, I saw them calling again, except it wasn't them - it was only Annie. She was in tears. She said as Evelyn was getting out of the car for school she looked at Annie and said, "That's my real dad, right, Mommy?" I knew then I would never let that kid go again, and I was leaking from my eyes too.

We would continue Skyping a few times a week. Evelyn was shy on camera, and English made her nervous. Everything made her nervous. Annie administered as much translation from being on a choppy Web call and speaking a broken, simple mix of two languages concurrently warranted. I booked a flight the earliest I could. October 22nd though November 1st, 2015, I was going to be spending with Evelyn for the first time she'll be old enough to remember me. All the things I lost or gave away were coming back to me.

My time leading up to the trip, I was a purely aglow. Life was balanced for long enough for me to believe I was capable of it. Prior to the last two years of my life I seriously doubted I would be capable of the life I was living. With Monica, I couldn't have asked for a more supportive partner at the time. She loved me beyond self-seeking and would have helped any way she could have. My employer sent their congratulations and acknowledgment of my efforts on and off the job.

Flying out in late October 2015 back to Bangkok, where I had never found even a small stretch of success worried me for some reason…who knows? I remember 'the other guy', my addiction, chiming in with his thoughts. I squashed them regardless of how loud he got.

Annie and Evelyn were agreeable with meeting me at the airport. I was more nervous than any other moment in my life. I mentally prepared myself for the apologetic tone of Annie's voice or the meek Asian disposition of Evelyn. I even prepared myself for

Evelyn being too shy for an emotional greeting. These thoughts swirled through my mind over the course of the twenty-six-hour journey. It didn't change the fact that I was going to squeeze the shit out of her. Walking down the gate, I have no words to match my feelings. Altitude does weird things to the body, but my senses all came back to me after my breath left me for a moment. I saw Evelyn standing behind Annie in the arrival's lane of Bangkok's airport. She didn't see me, but when I was close enough for Evelyn to recognize me, she leapt at me with all her force, and I squeezed her until I almost cracked one of her tiny ribs. She clung to me the entire way to my hotel, which was minutes from their home. I brought two suitcases. One, or should I say half of one, was my travel belongings, the other one and a half were gifts for Evelyn. She dove in the minute the bags hit the floor in the hotel. She leaned over and asked Annie, "Can I sleep with Daddy tonight?" I gushed. Annie didn't hesitate to say 'no' because Wally was not agreeable with me spending a night with my own child. What a dickbag. The following day we would be going to a water park. I told Evelyn maybe another night. She was devastated and in tears. I had no idea what to expect that night, but Evelyn made it clear she'd never be leaving me again, either. I had no idea if Annie would stay or leave when we got to the park, nor did I care. We set out in our bathing suits the next morning when Annie came to pick me up, Evelyn with her. I could hear Annie's phone ringing incessantly throughout all our rides during that trip. Wally was an insecure clown. That would be his emoji in my phone if his number were saved. He would scream at Annie when she answered and ask her if she was alone with me. Baby shit. Total junior high drama. I was kind of happy they were living this way though.

Annie walked us to the gate of the park and said goodbye. Everything with her was measured. If I had asked if we could have the day to ourselves, she would have suspected something and said no. There was nothing to suspect. I was clean and deserving, and even more so, Evelyn deserved the best version of her dad.

We went straight for the big slides and tube rides. The park was cheesy and something out of a National Lampoon's movie, but it was our first time together and wouldn't matter where the fuck it was or how fun or packed it was. We had each other, and I could feel a sense of contentment from Evelyn I never expected. I felt her innocence and I felt her pain in not knowing me. I felt every feeling she had. She would jabber on incessantly in a mix of Thai and English. She had so much to tell me. We had been talking on Skype about her interests and dreams, her daily life and schoolwork, but spending that day with her made me realize how impersonal a Skype call can be. This girl needed me, and she made it clear from that day on. It scared me and elated me. We sat and ate fries and talked in our wet suits. I talked to her like I did in the Philippines, except now she could respond, and she had no issue offering her opinions. I don't dare use the apple/tree cliché, but c'mon! We could both talk a cat off a tuna truck. I would go on to find there is a lot more than nature to thank for our children's characters and idiosyncrasies. We sat there goofing off and being what we would always be from the first hour we spent in Bangkok that day…best friends.

That night when we got in Annie's car to go back to the hotel, Evelyn slept on me, drooling, and I carried her up to my room when we pulled up with Annie's consent that she could spend the night with me. There was and never will be a minute with Evelyn I would turn down. No game, or play, or parent meeting. I had enough days off from this amazing little human to last ten lifetimes.

We spent morning to night together the entire trip and, in spite of Wally's orders, I spent a couple more nights with Evelyn. Evelyn sang, "Let it Go" on her Frozen microphone I bought for her most of the time. Her singing voice was more than offensive, but I didn't care. She was more comfortable than I could grasp. No one I had ever met was that instantaneously comfortable with me. There was nothing I could do wrong to this kid. She laughed at everything I said and wanted me to hold her hand and even carry her almost everywhere. Having missed those years where she was more appropriately sized for carrying, I didn't mind making up for that lost time. We went to Yo-Yo Land, a toddler-to-ten-year-old arcade and play zone, and we painted pottery and dug up fake dinosaur bones. I felt like a dad for the first time in my life. It was overwhelming. I was overwhelmed.

I couldn't ever be comfortable with nothing but great things happening in my life, so, in true Matt Garon fashion, I put a reservation in my mind somewhere between the time of reconnecting with Evelyn and flying there that October to let 'the other guy' out for a night. Life was just never meant to be this good. During the second to last night of my trip October 30th, 2015, I relapsed in epic style with crystal meth and three escorts. Shame on me…fucking shame. This was the moment my disease scared me more than any other point in my life.

I knew the misery it would bring. I would never know the length of time I would have to endure it. I used because 'the other guy' told me I would be fine. He justified it by wooing me with flattery of my accomplishments, the unavailability of meth back home, and as always, I deserved it. There isn't a single unquestioned minute that goes by on the way to Soi 3. I wasn't seeing Evelyn until the evening for trick or treat in an American village in Bangkok since it would be Halloween. I hated myself for being so unprepared.

That drug-filled, euphoric night would bring me right back to square one, with a growing reservation to let loose on my trips to Evelyn.

I gathered myself to get ready following my binge before Halloween with Evelyn. The moment I saw her smile and saw her overlook the drained look on my zombie-like, painted face, I stopped hearing 'the other guy'. He, too, was defenseless against Evelyn. Evelyn, dressed in the Elsa costume I'd bought for her a few days before, didn't care much for trick or treating that night, but she was never off when it came to her loving every minute we spent together. We went back to my hotel early, and I told her I would be leaving the next day and most likely back to see her after she turned five. Evelyn was quiet that night, and I was too, but we slept nose to nose and enjoyed our last night. I was not going to let 'the other guy' ruin my life. Not that night. He had his fix.

Heading back to Boston, I was just as aglow as leading up to the trip. I had done what I set out to do. Evelyn was more amazing than anything I had tried to prepare myself for leading up to the trip. Her automatic comfort and vulnerability were gripping my heart. She was so sweet, and granted, she has half of Annie's DNA, it almost made me cry at how mindful and courteous she was. I thought about how she would ask me to give squatters coins if I had some and if she could give away her Halloween costume to her smaller friend to wear next year - both things that would never have come up in my mind. I knew I needed her just as much as she needed me.

I landed in Boston with Monica awaiting my return in the cell lot at Logan Airport. We sat there talking about the trip. She loved seeing my happiness talking about Evelyn, as much as the neighbors would explain my own parents' glee in boasting about me and my athletic achievements growing up. I could see where the embarrassment was necessary. I could and would gloat about my amazing daughter whenever I got the chance - it's tough squeezing a compliment out of me in general, so this took some time for my people to get used to.

I was smitten, and despite a small relapse, I was back onto the good path and doing my duties as a father and boyfriend. One hiccup in the timeline surfaced as I got back, and it was a reality shovel to the face, and something that really challenged my personal integrity. I was noticing that the second day after I had been home and had gone to pee, I had a swollen ureter, and my piss was bloody. The head of my penis was itchy and pus-filled and even crusty in some areas. I had a clear case of chlamydia. I panicked and called my doctor. This was the same doctor that misdiagnosed me several times – actually, he never has yet to properly diagnose me. But I love his laugh and his big personality, and in times of desperation, his loyalty and understanding. In spite of Monica insisting I get a new doctor, a more qualified doctor, I chose to stick with him. He picked up the call after a long hold. I told doc I had no insurance currently active and that I had gotten chlamydia. He chuckled and even snorted while he was laughing a bit. I told him I needed some Azithromycin to get my penis back down to its normal, less swollen form. The second problem was going to be how to explain to Monica that after our "welcome home" sex, she may have gotten an unwanted gift that keeps on giving. I couldn't, could I? I had been mindful and assertive in having the hard conversations as they came, and it had done nothing but good things for me. The universe would be set back into balance each time. This one was a big one, however. Before hanging up with the doc, I explained my situation and he said, "You'll have two doses waiting for pickup at the pharmacy." Now all I had to do was find a way to get Monica to ingest it without knowing what it was for.

The next morning was Sunday, and I was getting ready for my weekly men's league baseball game. I thought it would be extra sweet of me to give Monica a wake-up smooch and make her a cup of hot coffee with a pinch of Azithromycin that day. She loved it, and me for being extra sweet and thoughtful. I was clicking my heels as I flew down the stairs and out the door at the crisis I had averted.

Round two of time with Evelyn would come the following June with eight months and a lot of Skype in between. Evelyn and I would do her homework and talk about things she wanted to do, what things are like in the US, and what we would ever do if she came here. Life has been sustained in compliance with its clean and happy terms throughout that year, and I would bring my mother with me to spend time with Evelyn too, whom she saw last when she was just days old, flying away from her drug addicted son and her newborn granddaughter following a military barricade at the local hospital for nonpayment of the bill. Things were better, and different, but we were happy having the time we dreamt of years leading up to it.

Landing in Bangkok in June 2016 was nerve racking on so many levels. It was eight months since I last saw Evelyn, and my addiction was at the forefront of my mind. It's too bad I can't choose my own head topic because that one would be the last one I opted to think about, but 'the other guy' was dying to get out. I tried to stay focused on the trip; we planned to go to the zoo and take Evelyn shopping. Earrings were fairly new to Evelyn after Annie and I discussed getting her ears pierced. Evelyn, in her earlier years, was almost always referred to as a boy. The earrings helped her lose the boy assumption, at the very least. The earrings would also be highly contentious when it came to changing them. Evelyn was scared. Her entire life to this point, I had to take into consideration, was led by two females who think every human is most likely a serial rapist and/or murderer. Every person is a potential for harm. This infuriated me. I believe it's the love and trust we emit that generates the best version of any human we come in contact with. This made it tough breaking the fairy tale stigma with Evelyn that pain is inevitable in life and there is no sense trying to protect a human from it. We are all given free will, and depending on the age and frequency we get to employ it is what makes us successful. I encourage going through hardship and pain in more controlled life learning settings. I'm very liberal, but I respect structure. Evelyn had been white-faced at the mention of changing her earrings. Tears filled her cute little eyeballs.

As Evelyn, myself, and my mother (Grammy now) got back to our Bangkok hotel the first night of our June 2016 visit with Evelyn, we had bought her bags of clothes and toys and a sequenced Elsa dress that she wouldn't take off. It was time to have the earring changing discussion. Evelyn scoffed at even the mention of it and went back to looking through her bags. I called her attention to it again, and again she blew it off. I went as far as threatening to bring that dress right back to the store, while tears poured down Evelyn's face...but I got them off, finally. It wasn't my greatest parenting moment, but a win is a win. The trip was as amazing as the first. I got to see Evelyn growing and learning and speaking acceptable levels of English. Annie had been supportive thus far and even thanked me for getting the earrings off. She asked this trip if we could go to sign the divorce decree. I couldn't have been happier, but I didn't know what to expect with the child custody portion of the divorce, and honestly, I didn't care. I felt confident that our bond, Evelyn and I, was indestructible. And, as an aside, not that either of us wanted to get married, but Monica was finding it odd to be in a three-year, committed relationship with a man technically married to someone in Thailand. Credit to Monica with a big relationship save there.

The second day of our trip, Annie pulled off an impromptu divorce just as niftily as she had pulled off a surprise wedding. She picked me up the second morning while my mother and Evelyn hung at the hotel to get acquainted. Evelyn and Grammy developed a special relationship that started that day. My mother, who had never had the opportunity to play spoiler before, reveled in the peace their relationship brought. She could coach and parent, almost without having to be the bearer of consequence. It was a reality my mother always wanted. It was beautiful seeing the two of them together.

Annie pulled into the Amphur in Bangkok to start the process. Annie told me it would be fast, as long as we didn't contest the divorce. I asked her what the structure would be to Evelyn's custody. Thailand only gives one parent rights. That parent can then decide everything for the child. In certain cases, the judge can issue joint custody, but even if that were the case, and the controlling parent doesn't follow through with the court ordered injustice, there is nothing the court can or would do physically to make that joint custody stick. Strange, but the courts and legal system in Thailand is just that. I was in a position all of a sudden to either refuse signing the divorce paper knowing I would need to concede my parental rights in Thailand and start the legal process, which may delay seeing Evelyn again at all until that was done or sign over my rights as a parent within the borders of the Kingdom of Thailand and ask that Annie co-parent amicably as we had been. I saw no harm in this, and more importantly, would never give up my time with Evelyn again. I did what I think most parents would have done and let right action be the light that led my way. It was an action that benefited Evelyn without my agenda. I had accepted these terms of visitation and felt myself being content with the father I had become to this point.

Monica and I were getting pretty progressively more and more comfortable with life, and each other: all the bills were paid, stress was something we heard about and never felt, drugs had never been a part of our relationship, and I dodged a major relationship bullet by avoiding matching chlamydia sores. I loved Monica, and in spite of a couple lapses in physical loyalty, I wanted to see us through to becoming a family. Monica, who was apprehensive about having another child on her best day, was starting to warm up to the idea of having one together. Children, as I maintain, are my dream and always were. Evelyn was the start of fulfilling that dream.

I grew up like most, assuming I was invincible and brushing off violent bangs and bruises, but the older I get, I can start to see the ante spiking on my life jackpots and consequences now becoming noticeable, almost instantly on a level of "God-fearing." I didn't gain a respect for my idea of God until after my fortieth birthday, but I was growing more and more in tune with the cosmic system of weights and measures that managed my happiness. Most of what I did after my mid-thirties had immediate repercussions. My usual passing thought to using meth in the States got immediately heightened knowing my drugs of choice were in heavy supply while I was in Bangkok. The second trip to see Evelyn brought more self-induced misery. I couldn't seem to ever get out of Bangkok fast enough before 'the other guy' got to me. 'the other guy', my addicted self, was patient, yet demanding, shrewd and well poised; I was anything but in my efforts to quell him. I ended my second to last night high, as was now becoming my modus operandi in the brisk, productive jaunts to build a bond with my daughter. It was harder leaving than the first time. I was expecting it to get easier. It would never get any easier. The obvious take away was that her feelings towards me were very strong. The less obvious take away, because it was trapped inside my head, was Evelyn's need to see the States. She had to know where I was coming from, who her cousins and aunts and uncles are. She wanted out of Thailand - it bored her there. After having another collapse in my attempted sobriety, I was starting to think I just couldn't be ok in Bangkok, ever. Leaving that time was absolutely the end of Bangkok for me.

Evelyn, for the second trip in a row, was devastated and unable to breath watching me go through airport security. We had spent day after night after day being inseparable. Evelyn and I talked about the kids in her school, the things she wanted for Christmas, and her thoughts on coming to visit me in the US, and most of all, being in the US for one of Grammy and Grampy's famous Fourth of July cookouts. Evelyn was ready. I was ready. I told her I would butter up her mother with compliments and cash in order to help massage her shifty agenda and perceived control and let Evelyn come to see her family the following year. Amazingly enough, Annie agreed. The summer of 2017 would be reserved for Evelyn to spend in Salem, NH. She was booked to arrive in early July, and after being the guest of honor at the packed cookout where she would meet her entire family that she had no idea about, we would fly to Disney World.

I had been working with the same company for three years leading up to Evelyn's vacation to the States. I had been promoted and had a traveling position, but there would be no one bothering me through Evelyn's trip. I had to fly twenty-three hours to Bangkok for one night to pick Evelyn up, because she was too young and scared to fly. I would have flown around the world three thousand times to have her. Annie and Wally had officially gone their separate ways, so the night I spent there we had dinner together - even Yai joined us. We joked and smiled. Evelyn stayed clung to me with her arms around my neck and her hands intertwined where her arms met, just behind my head. She would sleep that way most nights while finishing a movie or just saying goodnight to each other and drifting away. Our flight was leaving at four in the morning, so we all stayed together until it was time for the trip. Annie seemed unusually pleasant, flirtatious even, but I wasn't interested. We got to the airport and happily said our goodbyes for Evelyn's first trip and summer in the States. The moment Evelyn and I got through security and walked up to our gate were some of the scariest moments of my life. Everywhere I went I had another human dependent on me, dependent on my attention to her every hour of the day, and I so fucking loved it. I can't ever recall being too proud of myself for much, but that was one of the proudest moments of my life. Airborne over endless bodies of water with twenty-six hours of flying and layovers ahead of me was never sounding better than it did that early Siam morning. Evelyn and I went through every new movie release on my laptop. I never censored anything she watched or heard. I obviously have an affinity for four letter words and then some, so I figured Evelyn was already aware of whatever TV would reinforce. Movies were more of the same uncensored nonsense. It never even dawned on me to see if there was a full male frontal nudity scene in the first ten minutes of The Spy Who Dumped Me. This was the first movie and the last I would let Evelyn pick. I did not get nominated for father of the year that year.

We sat and ate, and we were ignorant plane slobs the whole way through the flight from Bangkok and into our Dubai layover, and then again into Boston. Evelyn wrapped up in her multiple blankets with headphones on, head swinging, and empty snacks and soda cans littered around our seats. Comfortable utopian bliss the entire ride outside of the cock and balls incident. We looked up the theme parks at Disney World, and we were both in agreement to use our fifth day pass to hit Animal Kingdom twice. Evelyn loved animals as much as I did. I thought about all the time I had lost, the pets I couldn't provide, the stolen bag on her first birthday, and I brought myself right back to the moment - still grateful, still with perspective, still with hope.

Gathering our bags at the carousel bore the same contented smile I carried from Bangkok. Evelyn trailing as closely as possible, we gave Grammy a quick hug and got on our way to Salem. We would have the night to sleep before waking up for the cookout, and then we'd be off for Florida the following day.

Evelyn was six years old and had never met anyone in her family besides Grammy at the time of her birth. She hadn't known of any of the one hundred and fourteen confirmed cookout guests. The cookouts are well run - my dad, Grampy, emcees the entire day, breaking away from the monotony of beer, swimming, and cards with things like steal-the-bacon, potato sack races, and egg toss. I am the youngest of a generation of cousins. My mother and father are both the youngest of their siblings - my father the youngest of seven, and my mother the youngest of four. My mother is typically my egg toss partner and has been for years, but since Evelyn was here and my mother, after forty years, still refused to take her wedding band off to play, Evelyn was in as my partner. We would lose miserably almost as soon as the game started, but I really didn't give a fuck. We were so high, existing with each other in our inexcusably obnoxious happiness. The support in numbers from my family is the true mark of what defines family. Evelyn was home - carried home by the prodigal son.

Our trip to Disney had a price tag well above my pay grade, and I didn't care one bit. It didn't bother me that I spent frivolously on park passes, toys, cotton candy, and whatever else brightened Evelyn's eyes. We were there to experience the wonder and magic. I heard so many nags after complaints scrunched between sighs of discontent. I reminded myself, as I'm sure all parents do, of the time

I lost or took for granted, my current state of gratitude, and I prayed that I would never take the moments I've collected as owed to me or unearned, because they all contributed to my "now." Parents whom had taken their privileges of parenthood to regrettable levels would surely never get to see the earthly rewards from patience and circumstance turning to opportunity.

Evelyn got no more out of the itinerary than she would with any adventure, but she got the adventure, and that is our purpose. I would adventure any day and anywhere with this girl, and we did. Returning from Florida, we would take our adventures out in road trips to Vermont to see reggae concerts, indoor water parks, sled parks, Manhattan, and wherever the days took us. She was a hard yes from the get-go. Monica would go on the short trips with us - she and Evelyn had a special bond too. Monica could provide the polish a brute like myself couldn't ever figure out. Hard work and precision were too time consuming for me, but essential to balance as a human. I loved them together, and Evelyn did too. I would sit back just to hear Evelyn communicate. I enforced her as a confident girl. Even when she had no confidence to work from, I gave her mine. I demanded she look people in the eye, greet them, shake firmly, bow respectfully, speak with purpose and conviction, and never disrespect another human. I shared stories at her request before bed. She would believe my magical journeys and make Monica listen to each one the next morning while I chuckled and went about my daily routines. Evelyn believed every word I spoke. I never felt more obligated to someone else's right to the truth, regardless of the insignificance of it. It was the truth, and all humans basic right to existence is that.

The month flew by, and before it was done I made sure to have an agreement in place with Annie to bring Evelyn back to the US in just four months for her first real Christmas. Evelyn, unlike myself, loves the snow and has been dreaming about the day she would get to play in some, build a snow fort, have a snowball fight, build a piss-tinted snowman with shades of plowed asphalt, or just sit inside and watch the magic happen. She was a snow bunny, and as much as I hate the snow, I would pull her sleigh if it meant her happiness. These were feelings I could never identify with prior to her hijacking my life. I love her being my assailant. Methamphetamine was a terrible villain.

The issue, or nonissue with a hint of earth shattering reality, would be Evelyn flying as an unaccompanied minor for her next trip. She tested the waters when I saw her off in Boston to head back with a chaperone to Bangkok to start her second grade year. That send-off was worse than the two prior, but I told Evelyn if she didn't buck up and get this trip done, she wouldn't be able to come for Christmas. I wouldn't be able to afford two more round trip tickets. Evelyn always bucked up when I needed her to. I made her, and she, in turn, made me. I didn't need to tell her why I wasn't going to Bangkok. Not yet, but I planned to tell her everything about me, good and bad. We were everything to each other.

Four months passed, and Evelyn and I didn't need to Skype three or four times a week anymore. We communicated when we could. We understood each other in spite of, and above, contrived formalities. We were cut from the same toxic cloth but gave each other everything we had.

She landed via a flight, traveling only with a chaperone at seven years old, to Boston and ran at me out of the gate with full force, crushing me with a cheek-planted, seven-year-old, flat-nosed, gorgeous squeeze that offers every pinch of vulnerability a dad could ever dream of. I melt still. It was my place in the world whenever and wherever she flung herself at me. She needed me, and she always will. She told me about the fancy lounge in Dubai and how she did like I asked and brought just an empty suitcase. She knew the deal - she would go home with two slightly over-the-weight limit suitcases for checked bags.

Monica was waiting to bring us back to Salem and start the countdown to Christmas, stopping at all the necessary childhood stops along the way. We drove around to see all the best houses laced in colorful Christmas lights, yard ornaments, and blow up floats. We made ugly as all hell gingerbread houses and ate all the chocolate pieces out of the Advent calendars long before Christmas Day. We covered our tracks, don't worry! Monica and Marley would pop on

Alexa to get some Christmas tunes rolling, and our days would take shape from there. I rank Christmases like most sick fucks; this was the best one since I misjudged my string of twenty-four wrapped regular Nintendo games back in 1986 for an accordion. Evelyn's happiness made a run at Mike Tyson's Punchout and Metroid that Christmas. Wink, wink. Please note my sarcasm.

Christmas Eve. It was getting close to shut eye when Evelyn gasped about not having her note done for Santa. These were the repetitious parent truths I had never experienced. I got it. She wrote her descriptive note outlining her acceptance of gifts she may not have gotten but were on her list. I marveled at her mindfulness and melted at the thought of her being a substantially and measurably better person than myself. I melted over her innocence.

Christmas that year at my family's home was as big of a Christmas as I could ever remember. Evelyn and Everly, my niece, tore into a mountain of gifts, carefully plucked by our life long fake Santa - Grampy. That Christmas we had Monica, Marley, Grammy, Grampy, Everly, Markus (my brother), Dee (the cunt), myself, and Evelyn. It was the biggest Christmas I could ever recall and the first Christmas to have that magical feel since I was young.

We would cruise in my beater 2004 Chrysler Sebring convertible blasting hip hop, pop, and reggae without apology in the frigid December air. She was seven, and we would duo her once favorite "I Need a Doctor" with Dr. Dre, Eminem, and Skylar Grey. I swore like a truck driver, and she was allowed full range of the English language so long as it was used in proper context and in the proper audience. I allow her to decide those standards and coach where needed. "The Bones" by Maren Morris - that was our "gay" song, as I ignorantly called it. She would fuck up the chorus as I fucked up my parts equally, out of tune and scary bad. I'll never use the term perfectly imperfect because I judge that hard, but it was our version of that. We actually sucked at singing. Evelyn was brokenhearted and refused to accept it when I told her. She also refused to believe when I told her unicorns and fairies aren't real. That's her problem now, I told her. I just asked her that she refrains from using those opinions at job interviews in the not so distant future. "Sure, Dad," Evelyn replied, nodding her head. Insert overflowing tear duct emoji now. Sarcasm is not a thing yet in Asia.

Sending her back was starting to get just as visibly hard for me as it was for her. Drugs were a memory and fatherhood looked so good on me. Evelyn and I were supposed to be together. We both knew it, but I did the right thing and returned her because that was now all I knew. We talked about getting her back as soon as school finished in June and having a longer summer. It was all we could do for now. Evelyn wouldn't come until the next December, and a lot happened between then.

I was happy as a clean, non-active addict, and I just removed the situations I seemed to not find success in. Bangkok was a situation I avoided. I was gaining traction as a national accounts candidate at work, and Monica and I just decided we would be ready to have a baby soon. She was undecided for the three years we'd been together and, after seeing the love and effort I put into Evelyn, was on board for baby Garon! We had gone through three years of happy life and were comfortable knowing we would be each other's lasts. Last pussy forever? This was always the negotiating stalemate for me. I didn't want to think that far ahead, and I wanted to stay with Monica, so I laid my worry to rest with the mindfulness, awareness, and power that come from living in the moment. There's a way of saying just about anything coercively, but we didn't need to massage our agendas. Moment to moment seemed easy - it was the thought of anything beyond that which caused anxiety and doubt. Living in the active mindset of each moment is the only way to eliminate and insecurities and projections. I was first to get moving on the potential new addition and made a date with a urologist. After jerking off into a cup and dropping it off at the hospital a few times, the doctor eventually called in late January of 2018 with good news. My sperm count was adequate enough to produce a little one. Monica was happy and had been off birth control for over six months already. We weren't the type to monitor ovulation; that only happens when couples sex lives are compromised. We had no reason to ever need a prompt to get busy with our feelings.

February of 2018 meant Monica and I would be heading to

a Connecticut casino and then shooting to Broadway in Manhattan for the Lion King for a Christmas gift weekend we had planned. We always had fun date nights, comfortable silences, and perfectly synchronized, role specific duties. We were harmonious as a couple - there was never anyone denying that. We spent every day together, and outside of my trips to Thailand, every night. It was that weekend trip where we would conceive what would be both of our second child.

We realized at some point in January that we, or I, had booked our getaway weekend with the Super Bowl going on and our hometown Patriots and Tom Brady were playing in it. We raced home to catch the second half of the game that Sunday after the Lion King. Tom Brady willed the Patriots to victory after trailing by twenty-five points, and everything just seemed to be in line. I would be naive to think anyone needs a thorough explanation as to what usually happens next...

Just before Evelyn's seventh birthday, in late February of 2018, Monica noticed she was late, and for me, that meant incredible news. It had been just over a month since we'd heard from my urologist. Our weekend was behind us and the life of parents ahead. The pregnancy test came back with two sharp lines. We were having a baby, I thought.

As the weeks moved along, three to be exact, we were

talking less about the pregnancy, and I could see there was apprehension in Monica's tone. Her face just didn't sell me on her wanting the baby at that moment, for good reason. Evelyn knew we were trying through our Skype calls and knew we had a positive pregnancy test. She was beside herself with happiness. Playing with a younger autistic sister is rewarding and fun, but there would always be a disconnect. I asked Monica if there was something going on, thinking maybe she was getting hormonal a little prematurely. I would say that the moments leading up to that one, and just up until that one, were the successive best moments of my existence.

Within minutes of asking Monica if there was something going on in her head, she came to tell me what exactly it was written all over her face.

"I had an abortion this morning," Monica said nervously. "I'm just not ready to have a baby, Matthew."

I just turned, and turned, and turned inside and out. My belly and head took on different levels of raw emotion, none of which felt good. I disappeared to the bedroom to figure out what I just heard. I had to digest the words and the experience of what Monica was going through to push her to kill an unborn child without even a discussion. I was ready to self-destruct. I was angry and dead inside. I still feel it today. This was the final chink in the chain. It set me into the swirling vortex that I couldn't stay away from - active addiction.

I picked up some crack cocaine from a former employee. I ran into him leaving the poker hall while trying to avoid the emptiness at home a couple weeks after the abortion. I welcomed the situations I prided myself on avoiding. Darkness had taken most of what purity I had left after the abortion. I would begin using crack, weed, cocaine, pills, and fentanyl again to substitute my unavailable drug of choice. Part of it was clinging to the abortion, and part was that I am and will be an addict until the day I die. Monica went back on birth control and refused sex most nights. We would mouth the words, "I'm trying here," without ever really knowing what they meant. We couldn't do what we didn't feel.

We were equally as hurt to be where we were, but I blamed Monica. She would call my faithfulness into question unfairly and desperately try to find a way that it could be my fault, but it wasn't. I tried immensely to understand her. We were in our late thirties, we didn't own our home, and we didn't have any other children together. All things stacked up and still nothing I could find was worth killing a baby for. We were both guilty, but I took it personally.

Over the course of the next six months, I would use whatever fucked me up the most as recklessly as I could. I'd be out all night high and driving around, getting arrested, and ultimately ending up in rehab. Monica had helped move me out of the house once my run was over. My employer was still unaware of my progressively nauseating decline and urged me forward. I was always a well-functioning junkie. I ultimately started that tour in rehab by informing my boss, and the owner of the company, that I had steadily stolen from my accounts and accumulated a $48,943 debt with him. An IOU wasn't going to cut it, but in exchange for not sending me to prison, I would do a thirty-day inpatient program in Ashby, Massachusetts and return to the company to pay back my debt while taking a demotion. I was grateful. I never even took into consideration during my run how all this was going to affect Evelyn's next trip, which was less than two months away.

I spent a month in October of 2018 watching the Red Sox win the World Series from a rehab couch. I was grateful it wasn't from prison. I managed to master ping-pong, stacking rocks, horseback riding, sharing my feelings, and yoga in my thirty-day spiritual getaway. I probably didn't master them as much as I thought I had, but I'll live in the ignorance. I cleared up in those thirty days. The run was behind me.

Monica did come pick me up from rehab. We were still friends. Neither of us really wanted to admit it, but we were always better suited that way. I had worked through a lot, and so had she.

She dropped me off at my new home, my family's house just across the lake from where Monica and I lived. It was also occupied by my brother, mother, father, sister-in-law, niece, and newborn nephew. I would stay in the finished basement until I could get things together. I was still employed but working off a massive debt. I was working an hour and a half from home, making thirty percent less money, and in early sobriety again.

I would drive out to Worcester, MA, my least favorite city. It is overrun with opiates and crack. I drove those one hundred and eighty miles a day with less than enough money to cover the gas and car payment during a nasty winter. I wanted to do the right things, but I was building a resentment from feeling trapped and inadequate. I was failing in my newest role, and, in all honesty, neither I nor any employer I've ever worked for had an issue with my performance. This was new, and it was my built-up resentments not letting me put everything into the right thing. I wear everything on my sleeve, and I haven't a clue how else to do it. There's no surprise or subtlety. As much as you'll be able to see my enjoyment of something, you'll be equally able to see my disdain.

Christmas was going to be a quick visit from Evelyn. Even though it had been a year since I'd seen her, and it was a year I needed her. I needed myself again first. I was working as much as I could to pay for Evelyn's school as well. Her tuition for second grade was around twenty-five thousand dollars. Her school had taken the kid's school Winter break down from three weeks to two. I was disappointed and looking for a reason to quit my job, but I wanted to work through my poor decisions and honor my commitment to paying back my debt. Integrity was important to me. Last Christmas was her first, and it had been epic, and in reality, probably would never be the same again. That's the same feeling our addiction chases - that first high times one hundred.

Evelyn came, alone on her own again, for Christmas, and I stayed clean. She inspired me against the worst person I know, my addicted self. That voice was never in my head when Evelyn was around. We took trips to Monica's house to exchange gifts. Our separation was new to her, and to me. I knew Evelyn would benefit from a female presence, so I used whoever was around: Dee, my sister, Grammy, and a couple female friends Evelyn took a liking to. One friend was Michelle, who went to prison for a year shortly after meeting Evelyn and kept involved in her life enough to have spent time since her release, sent Evelyn the niftiest infinity scarf as a Christmas gift to Evelyn while in prison, and served as her last hairdresser since her release. The other was Francesca, a Dominican ex-girlfriend that constantly told Evelyn how beautiful she is and was always rubbing her hands over Evelyn's face like she couldn't believe she's real. Monica was a steadier influence shortly after our separation, but grew apart from Evelyn as we did in customary grief chart form. We finally hit the acceptance portion of the program.

Evelyn was starting to really develop a Western, less submissive personality. She was learning from being with me. She wasn't afraid of everything anymore. I could see her practicing speaking up and looking people in the eye. She was well spoken. I was proud of her. I knew I'd never be able to teach her how to be a female, so I didn't try. I have no problem saying I'm unqualified in that instance. We spent our time together regardless of who else was around. Evelyn would stay over her friend's houses for sleepovers, as long as they were my friend's kids, of course. That was something Annie would never allow. She had more friends in her four total months spent in the US than in her seven years in Thailand. She was connected every minute of the day to other people while she was with me, but she spent her time alone in Bangkok. She told me Annie rarely speaks to her and has never had a heartfelt conversation. I could see that. It bolstered our connection even more. We went on fishing trips. In fact, no less than three seconds after Evelyn first dipped her work rigged line in the water she had a perch. I was just wrapping up my talk about the patience needed to catch a fish. Fuck my life.

We did summer things in the summer: fireworks, cookouts, arcades, go-karts, and camping. Evelyn has an affinity for a glamping ground in the White Mountains, New Hampshire. They have dodgeball games, where I wreak havoc, water slides, a stocked pond, and my favorite glamping must have - electricity in every campground. I did whatever Evelyn wanted to experience on repeat.

It was time to see Evelyn off. I just passed the eightieth consecutive day of sobriety. It was harder than any time before.

When our addiction gets arrested by force, it's hard for the mind to accept that it was the right time. The brain clings to the reservation it has to use regardless of how much time has elapsed. It stays with the entitlements of going out on our own terms. Our addiction suffers from pride as well.

I was feeling better about my job and the path I chose, the path of high integrity. Evelyn and I, as was becoming customary, had a complete breakdown at the airport. I struggled staying dry when she opened up and the reality of the fact that the next date on my calendar we would see each other again was the furthest away it could be from that moment. It struck me the moment she disappeared through those gates.

All the time lost over three and a half years felt like a distant dream. I had my Evelyn back. We spent our time, and we answered to no one. I never wondered what other kids and parents did. I mean, the basics of having a daughter by my side, dependent on my planning and execution I inherently had developed. I kept her backpack stuffed with fresh clothes, bathing suits, elastics on my wrist for when she lost hers, chapstick (which I hate), water bottles, gum, a snack, tissues, sanitizer, bandages, her nasal inhaler, and anything she was currently into to keep her busy if our day got long. Apparently, if you have kids, this setup and the maintenance of it will get you far. It's like the 'how to grow a kid' startup kit. My kid was growing, and so was my ability, in light of all my faults, to take care of her how she deserved.

I mentioned I didn't know how to raise a female, but I made sure we stopped at all my female friend's houses so Evelyn had ample time to see how the other species, women, lived. I would hang tight and let Evelyn get some time with dolls, or opening a fake ice cream stand where I was the only pretend customer. I ad-libbed through several plays where I was the guest of honor or my role adapted to either a pet or even an inanimate object. I played hide and Hatchimal doll seek, danced to Disney songs, played with American Girl dolls, and saw every new cartoon animated release on the day it hit the movie theatre. We watched tons of movies and both referenced them by quoting the lines we remembered, which were most. I was raising her in my time the way a parent should. People, mostly because I don't have a vagina, would compliment me for being a good dad. I think that it's normal to be a good parent. I'll never understand how someone isn't completely obsessed with the mini version of themselves - maybe because they don't like themselves. I didn't like myself too much, but I couldn't dream of not wanting so much more for Evelyn. 'the other guy' was my least favorite two-legged mammal, without question.

Work never came around. I had been the golden boy for so long, but now I was just a martyr for my own cause. I grew disgruntled, and my boss took notice. I would be relieved from my duties in early April 12th, 2019, six months into my sobriety. That was the date I relapsed for the last time. That's not to say I used every day - it means my mind was addicted, my behaviors often showed it, and my drug use perpetuated it. We don't know we are removed from our addicted self until we've had enough clarity to know which version of ourselves, we are dealing with.

One week before my admitted collapse five months prior I was shaking hands with my company's owner at our annual company pow-wow about my next promotion. His exact words were, "Never have I seen a star rise as quickly in this company as you, Matt." His last words were, "We will no longer be needing your services, Matt." I was still trying to dig my way out of my brother's basement, and I was going backwards. I make no excuses - it was me trying to escape myself. I knew better. By the end of the night 'the other guy' was celebrating having dodged the remaining thirty plus thousand dollars on my bill. I was back to the bottom in one night, and I kept digging.

That night I found meth in the States. I heard about the West Coast having an abundance of meth and problems, so I stuck to the East Coast. I never asked a dealer or mentioned to anyone I dealt with in my running as to where I could find any. It scared the shit out of me. As I was laying down to bed one night after a long crack binge, I was at the point of hearing the loser birds about to come up and start chirping, when my friend Deanna started texting. Evelyn was still weeks from coming and my addiction told me there was plenty of time to get it together. I got up to see what the fuck she was on about. She knew I loved meth and met a guy a few towns over that had some. It was my greatest fear and biggest wish from each of the people inside me. We picked up a half gram after the sun came up to kill the high from the night before. I was alive again! Well, 'the other guy' was, and it sucked.

That same month I turned the corner back towards hell, free-falling, Annie called with Evelyn in the car. School was a few weeks from ending and Evelyn's summer trip was already booked. I was a hot mess. They weren't calling to discuss any of that, however. Annie pulled the camera towards her face and said, as if she had rehearsed this several times, "Do you think it's ok for Evelyn to go live with you?" I was blown away. What? How? I didn't get it. I immediately thought about the fact that I was high, and it hurt me. I needed to be ready for this. I don't think there was ever a time the word "no" was less likely. I knew I had hit a patch of heavy addiction that had little hope, but she was my hope, and I was hers. Evelyn was going to come live with me, for good.

11 | ADDICT OF THE YEAR - 2018

May 28th, 2019 - Evelyn arrived off a chaperoned flight that was paid for by my mother in exchange for moving them and avoiding having to pay professional movers. I justify my mooching as if it needs it. I had a newly raging, resurfaced, active addiction, and it was to meth, again, in the States. I was fucked. I had put immeasurable, unnecessary pressure on myself, looking back. As a matter of fact, my addiction did, but I am responsible for him too.

I was trying and staying clean when Evelyn arrived. She had just turned eight and it was, as she will joyfully recite, the happiest day of her life. Evelyn and I arrived at our first home together. The first time we could really call it "home" - a basement studio where she shared a bed with her dad and watched TV in a room without windows. My head was angry when it should have been content. I wanted so much more for her. My mother was supporting what I could not. I had paid for Evelyn's life and international school the past few years, so that bought me time to fight 'the other guy' and helped me justify my current position as being a product of the cause, when really it was a product of my addiction. I stumbled often, but I kept trying. I tried every day, and I struggled. Struggle doesn't have to mean I used. Struggle could be having a clean day from drugs but allowing 'the other guy' to impose his will in any given situation. My reactive self, or my addiction, is never going to have a day in hibernation. It is knowing this that keeps me alert.

I needed to work. I would take a position as general manager and executive chef of a five-star boutique hotel close to home. Evelyn had just moved and was getting ready to start third grade. She hadn't yet been away from me for more than a few hours, but we were living with four other adults and two other children, now that James, my nephew, was born. Still, Evelyn couldn't calm herself down in my absence. Starting on the first day of work Evelyn was calling me at seven that night to ask when I'd be home, crying incessantly. All the time we spent together would ill prepare her for being there and trying to sleep without me being home. She would call me in tears every night. After about a week or so my addiction broke me like a frail little bitch. I let the phone ring while I went to the seedy alleys of Lynn, MA and got myself a gram to smoke. I used my drug as my out, my escape, to real life stresses. I used it as a cheap out to my real life as a now full-time, single father. I would leave that job and start looking for something better suited for a single parent. I agreed that it was most likely time to put restaurants and hotels behind me. They would never allow me to live the life of a father that I wanted. I struggled from that day on, for a couple years, but I fought it. I fought the withdrawals and efforts that my addiction urged me towards. I fought 'the other guy' and will fight him every day to stop the warring battlefield in my mind with a white flag. I surrender to him, and I am free. I tried action and non-action. I could hear the pure, authentic me pleading with him to stop, but he took me out to have his way with us while Evelyn would be consoled by her grandparents, making apologies and excuses when I wasn't well.

From the first day of third grade Evelyn was getting herself up for school, showering, making her breakfast, and getting on the bus. I was just coming down from the previous night's high. We were sleeping on the same full-sized bed in my brother's basement. She would come down and give me a kiss at seven and tell me to have a great day and she loved me. I had no idea who this kid was. She was my fucking hero, for one.

I compared my bratty, entitled, hockey snob lifestyle growing up to Evelyn's sweet and generous stance. My family was lower blue collar, but my parents sacrificed everything for us to play elitist sports and have brand name clothes. I wanted this for Evelyn more than anyone knew, but she always maintained that having me was just enough. She had the patient resolve of an adult. I think she knew I wasn't qualified, but she did her best. I wanted her to have everything she wanted, as well as a sense of mindfulness and generosity. She had it already. She was already a better person at eight years old than I ever was.

She would come home off the bus and start yelling for me, running down the driveway, every day. She was just as excited as I was to see her at any moment. She would tell me about her day at school - it was always "great," and then we would get into who did what, who was getting in trouble, who was not doing well in their work, and who she was making friends with. Evelyn could do whatever she wanted. I implore, even in my addictive mind, the importance of being a giver. We're born takers, meaning we look to extract what we can from any situation - training the mind only to offer what we can, relative to what's happening around us, is a difficult task for a taker. Evelyn got it, though. Being the species equivalent to eight million others is tough to grasp when the fates of so many are far worse than the one we were born into. Being eight years old but using those privileges to promote balance, warmth, and happiness through a mindful purpose was her basic human obligation. I teach Evelyn the importance of minding her business but to always be mindful and aware. I teach her to impose her will only when necessary and only to support progress and amicable resolutions. I teach her to be small, smaller than she probably thinks she needs to be. I teach her how to fight and let her MMA instructors coach her on self-defense, but only self-defense. I'm not opposed to physical violence if it brings a swifter resolution. I don't believe people should take solace in imposing their hurtful intentions through the perceived safeties behind the glass of their phones and windshields. I kept people accountable, so Evelyn doesn't have to. I brawled, because I'd do whatever was needed. I kept that kid safe emotionally, spiritually, and physically, and I taught her to do the same.

- I didn't negotiate with terrorists, and that included terrorists that targeted addiction and feelings. I didn't negotiate with them because they had already captured my allegiances. My thinking there was a negotiation going on was the sickness. I surrendered, so I thought, as it was the only way to be free. I'd been beaten down by a shard of synthetic rock for over a decade by this point. It was time to shit or get off the pot.

By the winter of 2020 COVID was on us globally. Evelyn's school had gone to home schooling in light of the raging pandemic, and I was slinging ounces of meth daily to support my habit, but she loved me still, more than before. Evelyn found compassion in taking care of me. I believe she knew about me but never wanted to admit it. I believe she prayed for me, as I would see her do when she really wanted something, despite having never been introduced to any religion. I saw her growing into someone I was proud of, if only I could have been proud of myself enough to get it then. Boo-fucking hoo!

The winter would see me accumulate arrests and nights in jail. My poor mother and father were left to handle Evelyn's tears for her father most nights. The worse my addiction got, the earlier the doors of my family's house would lock, setting up my night in my car. One would think that loneliness was enough to get home at a decent hour to kiss my daughter before bed and make sure her hair and teeth were taken care of, her butt scrubbed, and she was comfy and safe, but my addiction thought better of that. My family was protecting themselves, and Evelyn from me.

I, like most of the country, stood firm on using my state unemployment pool to support my quest as a father, when at the time, it was only supporting my addiction. I began working with a dog breeder to supplement my habit and passive income module. Evelyn loved the puppies that would come and obligatorily have to rip herself away from them when it sold. A necessary life lesson - we don't always get what we want.

I met a dog breeder from Michigan, a twelve-hour drive, and asked Evelyn if she wanted to road trip with me. She was a hard yes, so the weekend before her ninth birthday party, we set out. I set out with less than enough money for the dog and gas and a bag full of meth. I would stop at roadside rest stops to use in the bathrooms while nine-year-old Evelyn waited in the car, sometimes for thirty minutes. I handed her my phone with the navigation set to the destination address and told her she's my co-pilot. She was in her own little version of heaven.

As we made our way through upstate New York, I was too high to realize our literal path was set to pass through Canada. This would have been perfectly well and good, but I had no identification for me or Evelyn, a car that looked like we were squatting in it, and foil and methamphetamines scattered about, some in plain sight. As I apologetically approached border patrol, which has not been great to me in moments past, I explained my miscalculation and humbly asked permission to pass through, explaining that our final destination was Michigan. Border patrol, visibly pissed off at my carelessness, pulled us out and gave the flashlight check. While two officers shined up the car and as many belongings as they could make out, they asked what my purpose was. Evelyn interjected at the perfect time. "We're getting a puppy!" she bellowed. The border patrol officer laughed. He handed me back my phone after inspecting a digital copy of a lost passport and said I need to check-out and be exiting Canada via Michigan within the next three hours. We were safe, and Evelyn saved us. She saved me, seeing as though the only reason I am above ground post-forty is due to her existence.

We laughed at how dumb I was as we were passing through Canada for letting an eight-year-old navigate while on a twelve, turning into a thirty-hour, road trip, for driving over international borders with no IDs and a car full of drugs, and for getting a puppy to sell off for an eight-hundred-dollar profit. I was obviously not fit to lead this operation. That was further acknowledged when the exiting border patrol officer asked us to kindly not come back through Canada, ever!

When we arrived at the seller's house, just after midnight, I did not have enough cash left after our trip, and drugs, to buy the pup. Since it was a twelve-hour drive from home, I slept in the car with Evelyn and talked it up as being adventurous. I hated telling her I was broke. I hated being broke. I hated being broken even more.

We waited out a teammate from baseball to wire the money I was short for the puppy. I'm still clueless as to how I convinced myself this was a good idea. The day got long, and we waited in a Walmart parking lot in bumfuck Michigan. The sellers were exhausted at my excuses and ready to bail on us, even after driving all that way, which I wouldn't have blamed them for doing in light of how unprepared I was and with plan B taking forever.

Sundae, our Olde English Bulldog, as Evelyn named her, finally had her bail money sent and we were back on the road, the long way, to home. She named it Sundae because her coat looked like swirling chocolate and caramel sauces, and because we ended up getting her on Sunday. Through Toledo, Cleveland, Pittsburgh, and so on, we drove and stopped where we needed to, in order to get food and use meth. It was gross. I felt disgusting. We had been banned from Canada, had to borrow money to support my habit, and I had lied about it. This trip personified the type of father I hated being. That trip also took us right through March 4th, Evelyn's birthday, and we not only missed her party but allowed all the guests to arrive at the trampoline park I booked to host it without us being there. Arriving home at my brother's house after such a telling experience as to where my mind was as a parent and active addict was alarming. I was tired of living in that basement. Evelyn was tired of not having her own room. I was tired of being me.

My addiction didn't let me regroup. Sundae was sold off just after we got home, to Evelyn's heartache. I would have kept her if I had a home. Evelyn wanted that dog, or any four-legged animal, as a pet... so intensely. They snuggled each other while I drove back, never taking their noses apart. It hurt me to not be able to give these things to Evelyn, as I'm sure most parents would attest.

My family, God bless them, had been through over a decade of my abuse, lying, theft, and self-induced misery that always led to my crawling back. My mother and father, my once biggest fans, were left to question which version of me they were going to see. My brother, Markus, and I, who were once close, barely exchanged acknowledgments of each other's existence anymore. His wife, Dee, was officially done with me, not knowing the best could be yet to come. Their children, Olivia and James, however, loved me and being around me. They needed Uncle Matt, and they weren't shy about showing it. I even, in my worst addiction, would sit and slow my life down for either of them, and I proved it repeatedly. My addiction showed his weakness, or my authentic character drew a hard line in the sand. It's still unclear.

June 12th, 2020, was the mark of my final change. I would love to say it wasn't forced, and that everything that followed was healthy, but that would be a perverse lie. I was arrested by Salem PD for stealing a truck, possessing class-A drugs, and leaving the scene of an accident. I sideswiped a car the night before and ended up with a broken axle. I stole a utility truck from a highway work site and went to file my report at the police station from the accident. I pulled up to Salem Police Department in my stolen truck with a pocket full of meth and arrogantly claimed how I was wronged. I left the station knowing they would come to fulfill my warrant. Hours later my street, where my brother and family lived, were littered in blue flashing lights and state troopers along with Salem PD. They knew about the truck and fished the drugs from my pocket as they pulled me out of the house in front of Evelyn and over the hood of the cruiser. It was my lowest point, but even two weeks in twenty-three-hour lockdown in Brentwood wouldn't quell 'the other guy'. He is adamant in the face of everything. He has less shame than the real me has.

Being abruptly thrown in jail and forced into withdrawals is ugly. Knowing Evelyn was tortured by my being there was even more painful. She understood everything, yet still apologized for me, placed her high mark of hope in me, and did her best for her and us. I marveled at this kid's abilities. It's also magical, because it's the most grounding and leveling place for addiction. I did my two weeks and left with a new piece of jewelry, an ankle bracelet. The bracelet kept me clean throughout the summer. My bouts of clean time would lead me to getting too well too quick. My addiction noted my turnaround time to regaining traction emotionally and financially and used this as a bargaining chip to my use. He was a skilled litigator.

September 1st, 2020 - Evelyn and I moved into our very first apartment together. It was a lower income community in Salem NH, five minutes from the family, with red brick and a "project-like" feel. I put down drugs for her, and then I put them down for myself. If even a molecule of love or adoration or glow abandoned Evelyn for even a moment, I may not have gotten to that point. Scary isn't going through life not paying bills, rent, or life invoices; scary is waking up and knowing that a human that loves you way more than you could ever love yourself is depending on those walls, that furnace, that TV and Internet, and you're still not sure you're capable of providing them. We moved in and adopted Loka, a domestic longhair kitten, Evelyn's first pet and love of her animal life. We took videos and made-up games to play with her.

Evelyn was starting fourth grade, and she wanted to try a new school in our new district, while still in Salem. She instantly loved Soule way more than Lancaster. She had friends there and, in her mind, knew our situation was more permanent than Grammy's house. We were officially independent and doing our thing as father and daughter, the best we could. I would moonlight small jobs to get by while Evelyn started making real school friends and looking into sports. She played soccer on the weekends. She busted her ass because she knew it made me proud. She played well. She was excelling all on her own. I would love to tell you it all came from me, but she was born with what she has.

My experience academically was me shifting my way through grades and classes as unnoticeably as I could while never once in my life opening a book between my last class and my next class. Evelyn loved school. She came home and did every bit of homework, and then we corrected it. I have a high capacity and retention rate, but school was just not for me. School and compliance were instilled in her character. I was in awe. I would show her my level of commitment to her efforts by being at every game, club, practice, play, volunteer event, and PTA meeting. I hated them, but I loved how she loved me for being there.

As we approached 2021 with a magical first Christmas of our own being in the books and my addiction on pause after my ankle bracelet and prison stint, I felt a huge level of gratitude and freedom. The bracelet and courts saved me during that six-month stretch. I became a father then. I would be ready to work again soon. Evelyn was comfortable with life and was fine being at home alone with Loka while I finished a shift. Grammy and Grampy were coming around again, slowly. My brother and sister-in-law were still too busy being better than everybody. They were the ones locking their doors and imposing their will in my parenting. They would scoff at anything I said and clearly formed their opinions of 'the other guy' and acted towards me as though 'the other guy' was doing my bidding from there on out. They refused me going in the house and on certain floors. They had cameras placed at all their egresses to monitor my movements. They treated me like an addict, and I can't blame them. I can blame them for anything other than that, which would come full circle.

March came, and we had fulfilled our previous year's shortcomings and made it to the trampoline park, where Evelyn had twenty friends waiting for her with cleverly made gifts and cards for her birthday party. I took huge chunks of pride away from being a dad and doing "dad" things. I felt emotional thinking back to where the last year brought me, all the deep valleys and mountainous peaks considered. We would Skype Annie any time we were doing memorable things, which was becoming more and more frequent.

April 2021 had brought opportunity. I asked Evelyn how she felt about moving to Boston and trying our luck in a big city. She loved the idea! I always knew she would be better equipped for constant stimulation, as the apple surely does not fall far from the tree. There, I said it. We would plan to move and get a nanny for Evelyn until we knew exactly what my schedule would look like. She loved that idea too. Evelyn was always up for hanging out with females. She's stuck in my hell of heightened testosterone most of the time, so I got it. My next job was going to be based in Boston with a high end, fast casual concept. My driver's license had been suspended stemming from the year and a half long debacle that arose just before Evelyn arrived and ended with me in jail. The beauty of doing the next right thing is not having to worry once that moment has passed about the negative consequences and culpabilities to doing otherwise. My court cases dried up, and I was given minimal consequences, none of which would jeopardize my rights to fatherhood.

We moved in on a Sunday in mid-April, just as the college was getting ready for graduation. The city village would be empty and ours for the summer thereafter. We found an amazing three-bedroom house in the center of the Boston University campus and enrolled Evelyn into an academy for her final two months of fourth grade. These were things I could have never done while high or in the addictive mental state. Evelyn, somewhat disappointed at having to leave her friends in Salem, forgot about them pretty quickly and boasted and bragged about her new home, school, baseball team, pottery classes, drama club, school plays, ice hockey, street hockey, and just time at the park with me and our new puppy, Brady. I was proud of myself. Brady was our big-boy rescue dog, a mix of Great Pyrenees and German Shepard, and emotionally unstable in the most loving way. He was gorgeous and didn't get a few feet from the door before getting his strokes. He had a long, Shepard-like tail and what looked like a perpetual smile on his face. He warmed our home and added character to a small family that already had a lot of color.

We hired a nanny whom Evelyn seemed to really enjoy. The issue I was having was knowing this nanny personally from a seedy website I frequented while I was being operated by 'the other guy'. She was an escort in her other world, and I knew this. I was torn as to what to do. She knew me as well and promised to keep her role with Evelyn professional, but I ended up firing her on the third day of her nanny role. I couldn't live with unprovoked stress from my past. That nanny ultimately filed a grievance with DCF, who involved themselves and imposed themselves in our lives, laughably. We were doing things right, and the complaint was thrown out. I find this tactic a symptom of the bullshit our American youth thinks is of equal value to their butt hurt feelings. A child being removed, even potentially, from a parent for no cause other than vindictiveness over hurt feelings is asinine. We moved on, as we should, confidently.

It wouldn't be long before we were in full swing. I was working, and Evelyn was getting home at close to six in the evening from school. I wouldn't need a nanny anyway. I had just entered a new relationship for the first time since Monica and I separated with an old high school acquaintance, who turns out is my actual human on this big blue ball, Tammy. She was tall and skinny, driven and confident, pretty in every way, to me. She loved me immediately, and I loved every minute we spent building our lives around each other. She and her two kids, Tank and Ellie, would take Evelyn under their guidance whenever they could. Life was balancing on every level. Evelyn loved them and welcomed them as her own family. She takes everyone at her own estimate, and I applaud that. Evelyn enjoyed being the youngest in the group, with Tank being thirteen and Ellie seventeen. They complimented and coached the areas I couldn't. We became a family fast. Tammy slid right into the role she was meant for in Evelyn's life. She was a friend and authority figure because we didn't need titles, and because stepmother is scary for a commitment-phobe.

Evelyn and I talked about going on so many trips, but the first one we needed to get done was the trip to see her mother, as over two years was about to pass, and borders began to open up post COVID. We planned July 21st, 2021, to spend the summer before fifth grade in Bangkok, a place Evelyn spoke little of and had little interest in returning to. I would remind Evelyn twice a week to call Annie, as it never crossed her mind. I pictured myself being on Annie's end, so I made sure Evelyn was doing her part. Annie called once or twice weekly as well, but their talks were usually just before bed after Evelyn brushed her teeth. There didn't seem to be a strong bond, but I never questioned it with Evelyn. We would send Annie and Lea, Evelyn's half-sister, birthday gifts and photos of everything we were doing. Annie sent many private emails thanking me for stepping up and getting to the point where Evelyn was in advanced placement classes. I found comfort in her praise, never knowing it was all for her own entertainment.

Through the two plus years Evelyn had been with me, we broke down all the walls of her upbringing in Thailand. I encouraged her trying whatever she wanted, accepting failure and the feelings that came with it, and making decisions predicated on logic, not feelings. She grew so fast, physically, emotionally, and intellectually. I would speak to her as an adult without ever dumbing down my words or expectations. She loved being pushed. We would walk to her little league games and practices right from school with Brady and talk about her day, and she intently listened and asked questions about mine. She wasn't the best baseball player, but she loved the camaraderie and the fact that I was the coach. She held me on a pedestal, which motivated me, as unhealthy as it may sound. We ate dinner at our favorite fried chicken place and brought scraps home for Brady. I sat outside the Clay Room while she got muddy potting clay. I let her fail and let her figure out how to succeed. We were doing everything perfectly. Any parent-child combo of human we would spend time around would compliment our bond and congratulate me for such an amazing child. To me that was like asking a fire hydrant to stop being red. It was nature, not nurture, coming full circle.

July came and Evelyn, Tammy, and I were running around getting her ready for her trip back to see Annie. COVID caused a number of administrative nightmares leading up to the trip, all of which we circumvented. Evelyn and I said goodbye from JFK Airport, just after we spent the week in Manhattan together, on July 21st, 2021, at the security gate. Even though it had been over two years and nonstop daddy-daughter life and shenanigans, Evelyn still had a hard time letting go. I will shamefully admit I was a bit relieved to have some time to myself and with Tammy.

12 | BANGKOK – ROUND 3 – AUGUST 2021

The moment she headed down the gate to security, I missed her, and something just felt off. She looked back tearfully and squeezed her pillow as tight as she could.

"I'll see you in a month, nitwit. I love you!" I shouted from the turnstiles looking down the gate. "I love you, Dad! See you soon," were the last words Evelyn said on US soil.

Evelyn checked in at Dubai and was quarantined for two weeks with Annie upon arrival into Bangkok. I gave them space to catch up and fill in the last couple years. I thought that was the most I could do.

Meanwhile, I got on with my one-month hall pass and would use it to grow into life with Tammy, Tank, and Ellie, or that was the plan, at least. It had been a long time since 'the other guy' spouted off, and it wasn't long after Evelyn left that I was texting my dealer. Again, I was looking to take what my addicted self refers to as "deserved" fun. I went right back to the guy I was, 'the other guy'. It was brief and complete, and I hated myself. I hate that guy and all the negativity he brought with him. By the end of my brief relapse, I was getting an email from Annie dated Aug 21st.

"I have been thinking a lot about Eve going back to state. I have lots of concerns, 2 times DCF, neglected, it's hard to decided that Eve stay in Thailand. She will have international homeschooling as I can effort. You can come to visit her anytime and about visiting state will plan again later. - Annie"

It's hard to imagine the feeling after reading this. Everything broke that day. Annie used me to space her bachelorette-hood to give herself a break from having two children. She waited like a serpent in the grass. I felt for Evelyn. Evelyn was broken, too.

As I hit send hoping for a response or rebuttal, Evelyn answered the call. She was in heavy tears, and I asked if her mother was in the room. She nodded, so I spoke for Annie to hear. I offered her citizenship and a life fully paid for in the US. I just asked that she didn't take Evelyn's future away when things were going so well. Evelyn begged and pleaded with her mother. Annie hung up the call. From that moment on August 21st, I took a long, hard look at all our positions: myself, Evelyn, Annie and how we were in this position. I had forgiven Annie for the first time Evelyn was removed from my life, but there would be no forgiveness to anyone knowingly putting my child through unwarranted torment. Evelyn hated it there. Annie blocked me immediately following the call. I was lost, completely, again. I picked up my pipe because that was the only way I knew how to cope with anything this fierce. I was in uncharted territory as far as my emotions would argue.

That last high of my life I will never forget. I finally had it. I had started renting out my apartment to accrue money so I could go to Thailand and get Evelyn back. A transvestite and his girlfriend rented out one room and my meth dealer was in Evelyn's room. They showed me exactly what I needed to never want to go back all the way, not to that. Being Evelyn's father outweighed even the most fantastical fantasies. There is no substitute, nor will there ever be. The hustle and grind while high through the nuances of the day were now unattractive. Sex and lustful escapades were trumped by little league championships.

I came to on September 28th, 2021 and put down the pipe forever. I threw everyone out of my house, texted Tammy to let her know I was ok, and sat in my own thoughts and withdrawals for one week. Tammy hadn't given up on me. Everyone else not named Evelyn had. When I was ready to get moving, I moved, and I haven't stopped yet, and never will. I was starting the process of re-acquiring everything I had lost through my years of toxicity and soul singeing - driver's license, COVID vaccination, PCR tests, birth certificate, expedited passport. I was a train careening hard, on path to validation. There was no stopping me or the cosmic gods that controlled my fate. October 21st, 2021, the Thai government lifted the two-week quarantine for all foreigners that were vaccinated from COVID 19, thus, making it possible to fly right into Bangkok and get to Evelyn. I bought my ticket to go rescue Evelyn. November 7th, 2021 - I would fly out with a return of November 20th. Everything from that day in late September was on overdrive. I told Evelyn I would never leave her, no matter what. I told her if I needed to move I would with her, but she hated Thailand and the loneliness and emptiness that came with it. Annie was in no position to pay for international school, and come to find out, she couldn't send Evelyn back to the school I paid for during first and second grade because Annie conveniently "misplaced" over six thousand dollars of tuition I had sent. Annie also had no parental jurisdiction in the US, so she pretended to have her tourist visa denied several times when we tried to bring her to the States. Add in that my cunt of a sister-in-law, whose sole purpose was my demise, had been encouraging Annie to abduct Evelyn, for her safety, from a man that she loves to no end all because she didn't think I was well behaved some years ago. She was right, but her right to discuss that with a woman she met on a brief vacation ten years prior was a little more than I would ever expect. Regardless of the facts I became privy to, there was no chance I wasn't going to rescue that kid. That was the only option. There were no others.

I gained so much support through social media posts from longtime friends following our lives and our story. The universe wouldn't put a nickel in my pocket that didn't need to be repaid tenfold if I had been using, but clean and connected my energy spoke. Friends and acquaintances encouraged me along my journey, offering money and kind words. They were and are paramount to my story. They kept me breathing on some days. They are my people, and all it takes to be my people is kindness and good intentions.

My flight to Bangkok was a world of anxiety from the previous three months leaving my body. I had clarity and my heart was warm. I made up my mind to not follow through with my elaborate plans of kidnapping. I had to do the right thing. I reached out to Annie via email on the plane. I asked that she respect the efforts I've made and let Evelyn come home, where she wanted to be. Annie never answers a question. She questions a question. She did respond, which was grounds to celebrate. She was going to bring Evelyn to see me at my hotel once I landed, but she did not respond to my main request. I accepted the time, for now.

I read a shortened version of the Tao. All my reads and finally non-action was a viable option. I imposed my will chronically throughout my life, and I didn't want to jeopardize Evelyn never making it back, so I listened intently with my ears. I spoke less and observed more. My flight landed, and the next two weeks would tell me everything I needed to know.

I woke up the morning after my flight arrived. I started to feel the Bangkok I knew once upon a time. My addiction never had a successful moment in this city, a city I loved more than my own. I quickly moved past the thought. Addiction and its behaviors were behind me.

I opened my email and saw a message from Annie. Evelyn would be dropped off at eight in the morning at the top of the street where my hotel was. It was 7:44. I ran out after putting on my shoes and grabbed a coffee as I headed to Pahk Soi. 8:01AM, and Annie's car zoomed past me with no other passengers. I looked up and saw Evelyn across the road, looking frantically for me. The force she propelled into me at can never be measured, but there can't be more love and vulnerability in a single action. I was squeezing her, and we were home...again.

We spent the day laughing about her abduction and talking about what we would do once we got home - neither of us thought about anything else anyway. We just took to our usual conversations about everything going on, how things are going with Tammy, how Brady is and if he's chewing up her stuffed animals. If I've been taking care of Loka - as if we'd not missed a day. She fit into her American life so seamlessly, wanting nothing more than what she already had. She never expressed interest in extravagant things. She has a natural instinct and mindfulness, at ten years old, to ask about her grandparents, aunts, uncle, cousins one by one and intent on hearing the answer. She was better than the situation I put her in, that we put her in. She was better than I was on her worst day, and my best. I went to Bangkok, as Evelyn knows, only to bring her home, so we ended our first day making sure we were seeing each other the next day, which Annie allowed. Evelyn had her phone still, so we signed into a messaging app together so we could communicate. I put an Apple AirTag, a tracking device, in Evelyn's backpack too. Annie had blocked all other means. We hugged it out a while that afternoon, and Evelyn got picked up and dashed outside to meet Annie.

The second day Evelyn came right up to my room. We were going to the embassy to see if there was something we could do to get a new passport, but Annie would have needed to be involved. Evelyn was bummed. I asked her if she knew that if leaving without her mom knowing would hurt their relationship. I was not sure what the thing to say is when you're spending a day with your parent-abducted daughter after flying around the world with the intention of re-kidnapping her. It was kind of unique, but Evelyn confidently replied, "I know what I'm saying, Dad." That was good enough for me. I texted Annie to meet us at the mall near their home, and she agreed. Evelyn and I sat restlessly at Mega Bangna Mall in Bangkok awaiting Annie. Evelyn had a swim meet that night, so we were meeting at 4:30PM as Annie was coming home from work. We sat waiting, decided to order some food for all of us around 4:45PM. Annie was messaging saying she'd be late. Evelyn and I counted to minutes until 5:30PM. The food was cold and so was our fleeting hope of an amicable resolution. Annie came hurriedly in at 5:35PM and told Evelyn to get her stuff. "No," Evelyn said, as I then scolded her impoliteness. I interjected, "Annie, you know why I'm here, and what we want. I am bringing Evelyn back home!"

"Mommy, I love you, but I just don't want to be here. I want to be in America with Dad and Grammy and Brady."

Annie looked at me angrily and sidestepped the question. She ordered Evelyn to pick up her bag and get moving to the car to get to swimming

"Can Dad come watch me swim?" she asked Annie.

"Let's go, then," Annie replied.

As we got on moving through Bangkok, Evelyn in front and me in the back, Annie stared straight ahead and started to ask questions about my income and address. This is all information she's been given, but somehow now she's seemingly forgotten that I make ten times her salary and have a large, warm home, as well as school enrollment at a private academy for Evelyn. All things she has had no success in ever providing Evelyn.

"Not to mention her own, unshared room, a cat, a dog, a large family, and so many friends," I added.

Annie pulled over on the highway and told me to get out of her car. Evelyn screamed and tears started pouring down her face. "No, Mommy, please!" she cried and cried.

I reached my arms and head around the seat in front of me, gave Evelyn a big squeeze and a kiss, and got out of the car. Annie was obviously not trying to help any situation other than her own.

"Good luck tonight, baby girl," I told Evelyn as Annie floored the gas to peel away.

The situation was clear - there was no way Annie was ever letting Evelyn come home with me. I started to regret not following through with my kidnapping plan, but I knew that was my addictive behavior seeking a thrill. Evelyn needed us both, and even though Evelyn supported whatever means necessary, I had to lead her without breaking either bond she has.

The next day Evelyn Face Timed me the minute Annie left for work. Evelyn was home alone. She was digging through the house for her passports - smart kid. She recognized the same fact and resolution in Annie's tone. See, all the controlled environments in the world can't change nature. It is nature.

Evelyn found the passports. I would jump on a motorbike and head to the airport to change our flights. Evelyn's return flight was put on ice by Emirates Airlines…nice people. I headed to get Evelyn. Once I got our flights sorted out to leave that night, I jumped in a taxi, anxiously following the tracking AirTag I put on Evelyn. I had butterflies in my stomach the entire way. I still have them. I arrived at her secure compound and walked down the street tracking the blue dot towards Evelyn. As I saw her standing in the entryway to her Bungalow, Annie was screaming and holding Evelyn's phone. I knew our plan was compromised. Evelyn saw me and swung open the gate and said, "Let's run for it, Dad!" I couldn't help but oblige. If Evelyn says run, I run. I couldn't get her to run out soccer plays, but here she was ordering me to kidnap her, if I could keep up!

We are both quite fleet afoot, and we sprinted to the end of the compound where we were trapped by that old bag of bones grandmother of hers, Yai, and her entourage of compound security… waiting for us. Annie had called ahead and blocked us in.

Sobbing profusely, Evelyn said, "Please take me, Dad. Please" explaining to your ten-year-old that superhero moves won't fix this problem in a country I have no jurisdiction or support is nearly impossible. It had become sobering reality in that moment. I knew then we would have to handle this legally.

Evelyn explained to security that she was left home alone and felt unsafe with her mother. Pretty clever tactic, but in Thailand the mother always gets to keep the child. The one benefit we got that day was police ordered visitation after our skirmish took us to the compound perimeter. Evelyn maintained in front of police and security that she felt unsafe and didn't want to be in Thailand. There was nothing any one of them could do. They did write a report about the incident, and Annie agreed that Evelyn and I could see each other for the last two days of my trip - November 19th and 20th. It was currently November 14th.

I would go back to my room and wait out the time to see Evelyn. We gave each other the warmest embrace and I told Evelyn, "No matter what, I'm never leaving you." She smiled and kissed me goodbye.

I was feeling relieved to at least have a police report that clearly defines my time with Evelyn. I would wait, and sleep, and quell the addict in me trying to coerce the authentic version of me outside to Soi 3.

"Not a fucking chance," I said to that cunt. "You're who got me here in the first place." He got me everywhere I didn't want to be. "I'm done with you; I'm done with you." I laid him to rest, forever, and counting.

At three the next morning, November 15th, Evelyn's AirTag was traveling five hundred miles north near Laos, in the jungle. She took Evelyn away from me again! I popped out of bed and jumped, half asleep, in a taxi bike to the police station. Frantically explaining the report ordering visitation I had just received and imploring the police to do something, they all refused saying, "It is a matter for family court."

"Well, what the fuck did I have to wait here for with my crying daughter for three hours yesterday?" I asked. My pain and excitement and irritation were falling on dead ears. The report was useless. Annie fled Bangkok because my child wanted to go home. Evelyn is not enrolled in any school, has no income from Annie to support her life, no hobbies or friends, no stable home, no phone, and no electronics - and she's been taken. That moment of reality took everything I had. Staying clean in a red-light district after just losing my child, less than two months after my last relapse was and still is the defining achievement of my recent past. I did it, and Evelyn has officially disappeared, off the grid. I asked for help that trip, so Tammy and the kids, all of whom know my speckled history, waited up and altered their sleeping habits to help me keep myself accountable. I had to. They saved my life. I can't take a blip of credit for achieving what I proved previously impossible. Together we can, alone I cannot.

I retained legal counsel, the best and most expensive in Bangkok. Evelyn has rights, and she purports that America is her home; that I, we, are home with each other. These truths are enough to bring her home in the time it takes. Without my John Wayne impersonation or the addict in me pulling the strings, I'm left to my thoughts, which are now an oasis of positivity and hope. Hope that will go on until Evelyn is home and then some. Evelyn will be home! It's my purpose; she is my purpose.

The Duke of Doucheville

13 | THE BROKEN CYCLE - 2022

I'm no longer doing this to claim my sobriety, my twenty-four hours, my right to speak at an AA meeting, or my right to anything other than wake up and breath, check in as a father, and check in as a human responsible for his own child's right to breath. I wake up with a mindful presence of where I am, and where I hope Evelyn is. I love blindly and follow the path of heaviest resistance. I am accountable for myself every day before my feet hit the floor. Where I clouded the goal and who I let manipulate my head are swept under the rug and dismissed as irrelevant. There is a manufacturer of fantasy and conspiracy in my mind, and it's my job to identify and eradicate the thought. The relevance of my thoughts should be measured by the actions that immediately follow. There is an urgency in my mind that is, for all intents and purposes, not relevant or proportionate to the situation. The situation is knowing that Evelyn is somewhere in Thailand in a place she doesn't want to be and doing the best she can...knowing I'm not far behind. It's my own head placing the urgency there for swift resolution, but I am helpless and hopeful. It's my penance to cope and behave in "fatherly" ways, as the universe is always searching and holding me accountable for the most mundane moments of my existence. I acknowledge my role in how this happened. Every decent human has that ability. It doesn't make it right. Nothing ever will justify lying to and stealing a human. I don't hate any longer - hate is where our darkest demons feed their hunger, waiting patiently for opportunity, and for us to employ them. Having the purpose and intentions of purity, and then acting them out, day after day, is what will bring Evelyn back home. I have faith. I pray to any God that will listen, because I will need all of them to agree with my absolved penance. Evelyn's misery was not my decision, but I fully accept my role in it and am working through, emotionally and physically, the retributions to life I owe until the day she comes home. I just need her home. Home is Evelyn's happiest place and always will be. We are each other's home. That was felt in our Bangkok embrace, and every moment we find our way back to each other, emotionally and geographically, henceforth.

My life's mission is exactly what the universe has forcefully been trying to teach me while I regurgitate at even the thought of things like patience, due process, compliance, and progressive goals through achieved stability and balance. Things I hate, yet something I will do every day I'm lucky enough to open my eyes with love coming in and love going out. Everything is gained for me when I put down my fight, paradoxically. Evelyn's happiness, and subsequently mine through hers, is the only thing to gain anymore. That is inevitable.

The only time an addict can truthfully, in their own lucid mind, be sure when the decisions they were making are genuinely being made with the sober or addicted mind are once, and only once, they've been removed from it long enough to actually know the difference. The time varies in everyone; it could be the time between relapses, the rate of the mind's ability to heal, the substance of choice, the imposition of others that cause resentments stifling the process, or a combination of all said truths. That is the scary part. Knowing that there is a place, not a creature, that lives inside me that can obstruct my ability to know myself, to make decisions that are predicated on the authentic version of myself and the soul and integrity I was born with is inexcusable to the people I love and gravely painful, or potentially, to me as an addict. The inability to discern my own true self is scary.

We, addicts, are never supposed to say "never" when it comes to the projections of life beyond the twenty-four-hour frame we're living through, but I will. I will never touch illegal narcotics, alcohol, or legal narcotics for the rest of my life. The pain in doing so and the consequences they bear are way too heavy to even entertain the noise 'the other guy' makes. It's non-negotiable, forever.

Most of us don't make it back to our true selves and will always question if we are there through the process weighing our progress to that of versions past, not realizing the irrelevance of such analysis.

I'm getting there. Knowing all this comes from a man responsible for raising a girl with infinite love and hope and faith in him is alarming, I get it. How scary do you think it gets for me? I think it's common for most parents to question their readiness for parenthood. I did. I do. I think I always will. I'm getting better with that thought.

I've never woken up and thought to myself, Let's fuck over every person I love and that loves me back, ingest endless potentially fatal chemicals, distance myself from the rest of humanity, enter each situation with nothing but an insatiable thirst for my next high while my addiction forces me to convince others of my wellness. My addiction scares me more than it scares those I love, but they would never know it. I would never know it. The cycle is a cycle because there are no fine points or edges. It's round. There is no end. There is only reprieve. And the reprieve almost always seemingly lands us back in the same hell. There are no clear rules and standards of conduct. There is confusion and pain, discomfort at best. There is an elephant in the room, which I so openly detest. There is no hope, at least not in me and my active use and sometimes in my inactive addiction. I find hope in a situation or a moment. How am I supposed to encapsulate that moment forever? It's mine to figure out, and I am so flawed and undeserving as I see it. I know self-loathing is toxic, and I feel as though my burdensome nature through addiction was so fierce that it's not right to put my people through it in my sobriety. That is the cycle.

I get why addicts feel the need to go back. The drug is my master, and I am its servant. The ephemeral thought of being clean forever is one I know goes against the grain of my being and against the advice of recovery experts, so I opt for the road that becomes compromised between the two people inside me that says it's at least worth looking into. There is no semblance of balance and there may never be. The thought of going through life (and life is a lot longer than the "life is short" people suggest) without projecting beyond the day I'm currently grinding through is unrealistic. Immersing myself into the self-help halls and recovery programs without projecting, while reading the likes of Tolle or Bukowski and seeing a way to balance my addicted self... is unrealistic. Accepting the terms that my inner good implores me to accept is grounds for termination to this other voice.

Lots of us go that route, but I don't have to. At least not today. I just can't figure out which version of myself I'm dealing with. No matter how informed I am regarding frontal lobes, amygdalae, or hippocampi is irrelevant. Addiction has brought some of our greatest minds and athletes to an early grave. In retrospect, I was unable to get it. We are unable to protect our true selves long enough to give us a chance. There is no defense in my polluted mind to myself, and more importantly, to those I care about. It's the people I care about that I hurt the most. Cliché, but true in every addict's case. Those are the people my addiction sees as means to my end, and the end is inevitable.

The times I've woken up, or come to, resolute in my thoughts to be well that day and get on with life as I see others doing is countless. The nights I've bowed my head in shame thinking that this is the last time I'll feel this way is equally countless. Our "people" wait with bated breath when they come to a sense of defeat, paradoxically, because there are no other options. They mourn the living.

The moment my active addiction and crazy mind subsides long enough after the self-inflicted torture tells me, no, begs me to stop, and I'm unable to go on…yet still alive, I catch a moment of hope. I try to ride the hope. The brain is cooked…I cooked it. I have taken my talents out of the kitchen…I believe in connection, healthy connection, being the catalyst for change. Change is a funny thing. It's welcome and unwelcome. Necessary but resisted, and I know this, yet still I impose my will. The driving force will forever be the hope of the potential I saw in myself as a father and partner. Life, not substance, needs to be, and will forever be my substance of choice.

They say there is no love on earth that will and can save us from our addiction at the height of its attack. I'm here to prove that isn't true:

moment by moment, hour by hour, day by day, and month by month, my purpose is Evelyn. Her love for me, not mine for her, or maybe a combination of both, I guess, is what cripples me to the floor and surrenders me to the purpose. I can admittedly find and feel it. I hope it's less ephemeral than my addiction wants it to be. Time will tell - another fucking cliché. Fact is that the feeling her love provides is more than any drug, women, or combination of the two will ever provide. The burnt image and almost visceral thought, as much as that sounds oxymoronic, of the way she playfully scolds me, the look on her face when I open her door in the morning to get her out of bed, her undeniable passion for animals and their happiness above hers, or her perpetually infectious cheerful mood, plunges a stake in the heart of my addiction. It annihilates it. It sets me free.

ABOUT THE AUTHOR

Garon, a chef by trade turned author, chronicles his journey throughout SE Asia as a meth addicted, struggling parent. Estranged from his daughter…he recalls all the gut-wrenching defeats through his addiction and failed parenthood.